Much of a Muchness

David Coad

Published by Lyvit Publishing, Cornwall

www.lyvit.com

ISBN 978-1-914206-00-9

Credits

Written by David Coad

Produced by David Coad & Terry Lander

Edited by David Coad & Terry Lander

Published by Terry Lander, Lyvit Publishing

Artwork by Penair School Creative Club Students

David Coad Books

1. Vibrant Eons
2. The Land of Dreams

Front & Back cover pictures painted by Amelie Rowe

Artists

Sophia Duval, Lorena Ferreira, Beau Beames, Ysabella Caddy, Lola Beames, Amber Vinten, Izzy Webb, Caitlin Swan, Amelie Rowe, John Roach, Evie Attrill, Molly-May Brothers, Taya Coles, Anisha Rahman, Ella Jones, Nuala Sellwood, Millie Matthews, Lauren Reeves, Eliza Atkins, Claudia Duval, Louise Hocking, Hermione Scrimgeour, Clara Rose-Reid, Lola Claridge-Wall, Lamorna Swan, Izzy Seyler, Harley Weake, Tilly Stephen, Hannah Ellis, Daisy Smith, Agnes Wade, Phoebe Warner-Bailey, AmyBrigden, Hephzibah Wills, Alex Nettleship, Jennifer Smith, Charlie Monroe, Sam Brown, Hannah Edge, Harvey Reeks, Alesha Waniowski, Charlotte Seyler, Kaelyn Gendall, Poppy Dixon, Leyla Powell, Charlotte Garcia, Jess Bryant, Courtney Hosking, Lily-Belle Smith, Cerys Newberry, Jeana Stephens, Nora de Cominges, Emma Freudenthal, Saphira Neuber, Evie Noble.

Thankyous

I would like to thank to following people for helping me in the making of this book.

All of my Penair School Creative club artists

Terry Lander, poet, publisher, writer and runner

Amelie Rowe for her beautiful front and back cover paintings

My beautiful wife Clare

Foreword

This second collection of poetry has taken me 14 years to complete. I never intended leaving it so long but I guess life got in the way. My writing continued, however getting a job as a teaching assistant and setting up and running such a successful after school creative club at Penair School in Truro took so much of my time and energy that I forgot about my own personal writing and focused so much on my after school club. During that time from 2008 to 2020 we made and published 11 Penair school creative books and I had so much fun and energy that my own work was pretty much forgotten. However during the Coronavirus Lockdown and while making a Shortlanesend village book I revisited old writings and poems and was soon working on and putting together this collection of poetry.

The other thing I want to mention is the incredible artwork that is in this book. I wanted a piece of art to go with every poem as I feel the art enhances the meaning of each poem, and for that I looked to my own Penair School creative club, and looked over artwork from the past 11 years to choose from. Thank you all for your incredible art.

I hope it won't be another 14 years until I produce my next collection of poetry.

David Coad November 2020

Contents

"People naturally experience an unease about, all of this. I think most human beings think, **well on the surface all of this seems to be working but it just doesn't kind of sit right.** That's why people attach to this work because there's a sense of relief, even if it's melancholic, you go **oh my god somebody else gets it to, somebody else feels this sense of unease.**"

Roger Waters of Pink Floyd talking about their Dark side of the moon album in a BBC interview in 2007

Above the Day

One day, one night
New lives shine bright
A hundred sunsets, a hundred moons
Life's over, far too soon
A thousand dusks, a thousand dawns
Time and its dominion, over the newly born
A million months in a billion days
Life lives its life, in a billion different ways
A billion years, through a trillion seasons
Life on earth, without any reasons
Eons through space, eons in time
Spirits in the universe,
Forever yours and mine

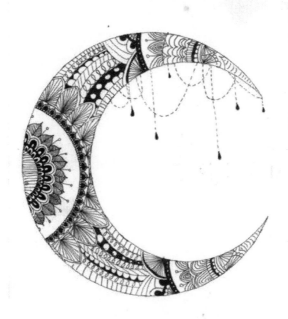

Over the Stars

Over the stars
To a land far away
Filled with music and song
Where children play.

Over the stars
To a city by the shore
Where you'll never be rich
And never be poor.

Over the stars
To a place in the sun
Cast away the bad times
To a future of fun.

Over the stars
Where we walk hand in hand
Spreading love and happiness
Throughout the land.

Over the stars
Join as one
Others will follow
Let them come.

Over the stars
Our tropical beach
Paradise at hand
Never out of reach.

Over the stars
Singing loves sweet song
Listen to your heart
You'll never go wrong.

Over the stars
Joining our fold
When you embrace loves magic
You'll never grow old.

Over the stars
Opening closed eyes
To a land where no none grows old
And no one ever dies.

Over the stars
To a place in your heart
Where only love waits
To paint its magic art.

The Stricken Maiden

On a wild and stormy night, she wakes me from
my sleep.
I creep across the room, and gaze out at the rain
sodden window.
There she is, just as before, all those times
before
standing, all in white, on the cliff-top
beautiful, fearful, desperate, worshipful
the wind tossing her long brown hair this way
and that
like the fields of overgrown wheat
the wind blowing at her wedding dress, up
and down
as she cries out in agony; her sad song
her sweet pitiful song, that will haunt
these cliffs forever.
I return to my bed, my soft warm inviting
bed
but I cannot sleep, for her desperate song
shall haunt me this night.
The rain lashes down and the wind howls,
distorting her song
her cries overwhelm it.
OH, poor child, if only I knew why you
grieve so........

He came to town, to rest and breathe in

the clean sea air
the beach was wide and open, and he
lapped-up the sun
then the day came when he saw her,
walking with her scruffy dog
treading in the soft warm sand, as the tide
lapped over her small feet
a white shawl, covering those secret
curves
rousing interest and passion that had laid
dormant for years.
He rises, and follows her.

A farmer's daughter. He will wait and
watch.
Milking the cows, feeding the chickens,
helping in the fields
his maiden was slim and beautiful, as he
watched with burning eyes
down on the beach, and up on the farm
her routine, as dependable as her smile
such a happy and gay spirit flowed from
her
friendly with everyone, and kind word, a
youthful laugh, and innocence
a prayer at church, a cuddle for the piglet.

He walked on the beach with the sun at
his back
the waves tormenting the gulls
her figure on the horizon, and the dog

running by her feet.
He walks towards her, with sea-shell in
his hand
he stops, as he feels her presence in his
soul
deepening his emotions of lust, passion
and love.
He throws the shell and steps on it
his flow of blood from his bare foot will
now drench this beach forever.

"Sir, Sir! Are you hurt?"
He looks up to see the face of an angel
the sun's rays glistening through her hair
as it waves and curls with the winds will.
Helping him to his feet, and hobbling on
his pretense, back to the inn.
The two stare at his feet, as the cook tends
his foot.
"Tomorrow, on the beach, tomorr……"
That night the wind grew in strength, and
the heavens opened
but no amount of rain would ever wash
the blood from that beach.

The morning was fine and bright, he was
beaming with all the joys of summer
he took up his place on the beach
the anticipation of her sweet being,
making him nervous
and so he took to the sea.

She came walking, feeling a strange kind
of weakness
for a woman knows deep in her heart,
what is man?
The handsome for the beauty, surrounded
with delicate touch
a feeling close to tears, yet tingled with
hope and a flutter.

A splash of salt water, a time gone
lost, like so many memories, never to
return
a broken promise that will be forever
there's.
"Where was he? He said he would be
here." Feeling of grief.
"Oh my lord, how long have I been
swimming?" Feelings of guilt.
A slow painful walk back
questions with no answers
a sad hurtful, uncomfortable day
an acted smile, hope being the final
feeling.

"But there he is, coming towards me."
"It's her. Thank the lord, it's her."
Yesterday's painful barrier, now melts
away with today's sunny radiance
for eyes will stare, waiting for the seizure
of captivation
hand in hand to a secret cave, dripping

8

echoes in the dark
a furry dog, barking and jumping
a touch of a hand, on smooth gentle skin.

Oh love, boundless love, exploding from
all pours, flowing in great passions of
energy
on the beach, in the fields, in the barn, in
the inn, in the woods
hand in hand, forever to be hand in hand,
forever to be a moment of the area
the courtship of the blessed, and the
downfall of the cursed
the price of love is risked, and the damned
shall never rest
to be joined in bliss, and forever smile
and cry-out in the darkness; the ravages of
a weary maiden.

To the instrument of darkness, a whisper
in the ear
a jealous dagger, stabbing at the fabric of
tomorrow
the flights of fantasy, turning sour, rotten
to the core
as the finger of falseness points unjustly
at her, his love,
affairs of the heart have only one bounty
and the price of betrayal, is unforgivable.

To the church, happy, crowded with the

joy of light
standing at the altar, awaiting her groom
the congregation mumble and fidget as the
doors open.
In he strides, not in his suit!!!
Her heart skips a beat, not knowing,
racked with fear
he comes to her and turns, facing the
gathered.
"She has touched another," he cries
pointing at her, as his tears fall
"She is a sinner...A WHORE!!"

Faces look on her, all at her, aghast
she trembles, desperately trying to
defending herself,
but the damage is done, its might
unrepairable,
she is unjustly cursed forever, swaying
under a torrent of spiked words that rip
her to shreds.
She runs from the church, crying, her
mind exploding
no knowing or caring which way she goes
just to get away, to get far, far away from
those awful stares, and hurtful words.

The day tarries, as she sits on the cliff-top
her life ruined, her name blackened for
eternity
her soul dead, her heart broken, her mind

numb, empty.
How could her love say such things?
Why was this happening?
The wind picks up and the sky darkens
the tide rolls in, on huge grey waves that
call to her
showing her the way out
and in the grey twilight, in the thunder and
lightning, and the pouring rain
with the salty sea air wind blowing a gale
she stands on the precipice
her wedding dress lapping all around her
in the gale
a tear is shed, rolling down her cheek, and
falling to the sea
a lump in her throat, as another tear falls
to the sea.
She breathes her last, and throws up her
arms in misery and prayer
"WHY?" She screams, singing to the
heavens
as the lightning strikes down, illuminating
her
a beautiful queen of terror, rising above
the cliffs, above all things
and feeling utter despair and relief, she
throws herself over the cliff, to the ocean
never to be seen again...
Until.......Unless.......There is a storm......

I wake and dress

the day is sunny, the sky is clear.
I remember last night, and the scene on the cliff.
I walk to it, with her haunting song still ringing in my ears.
I stand there, and something catches my eye.
There, on the rock edge, is a shell.
I pick it up to see blood drip from it.
Disgusted at the sight I throw it from the cliff top down onto the beach.
I thought nothing of this until another storm came a month or-so later
again she appeared on the cliff top, singing her beautiful haunting song.
The next morning I walked up to the cliff top to see that same sea-shell
just where it was when I found it last time.
Blood flowed from it.
I let it empty, and from it I hear a strange haunting sound.
I put the shell to my ear and hear her screams of agony and the passion of love between a man and a woman.
I throw the shell once more to the beach knowing it would not be the last time.

13

Minimum Wage

I'm stuck in a dead-end job on minimum wage
I feel like I'm trapped in a statistical cage
Doing a good job and working hard
Morning to evening, stamping my card
An insult to my intelligence and skills
Who are they to judge me, can they use drills?
No money for pleasure, weighed down with bills
This life just leaves me constantly sad with chills
Lowest of the low, looked down on from a great
height
Yet despite all, I have my pride, and they will
never blind my sight

Dark Polar

Eyrie Mountains of ice
Calling out to entice
Humps and shapes of centuries
Forever on epic time
Piercing wind of whine
Shiver in a sea of crystal
Giving up its colossal wealth
No one caring about its health
Its secrets now dripping away
A vast region of white
Distant moan of shifting weight
Taking shape in the day
Surface glides so far away
Enduring in a frozen state
Rising out of the gloom
Melting point, time of doom

Awake to Life

Awake mighty lord
Awake people of this world
Open your eyes
Look out upon your land
See the mighty deep forests
See the lush green fields
See the rivers that flow
See the mountains of might
See the sea that waves and crashes
For the curse has been lifted
The spell broken
The evil departed
See the deer that prance
See the rabbits that run
See the eagles soaring so high
All that is good has returned
Feel the wind on your face
The rain that soaks
The sun that shimmers
Taste the fruit from the trees
Hear the living of lives
Touch destiny which is all yours
Awake to beauty
Awake to living
Awake to life

The Neververse

Her face covered with ivory
Wash in water
Once my Bain
Now my daughter
Slender, beautiful and caring
Takes her place in the hall
Waiting for the painful call
Dimensions closed to the living
Opened to spirits and their giving
For as long as there is life
Pain and misery will run rife
Upon our souls, their hearts touch
Healing our bodies, giving so much
Dark halls of Valhalla
Open to the brave
Resting place for valour
Her beauty glides away
To the call from the fallen
Dawning with the day
To the man who has called
Giving up her spirit
To become a mortal
Her way back, forever blocked
By the magic portal
So I have lost my daughter
The one who saved her man and stopped the
slaughter
But proud of her am I
As I look on her with a knowing eye

Her life now complete with love, husband and child
Forever free, forever wild.

Molly Makes Mischief

With her curly ginger hair
And her freckles singed so fare
Her socks rolled down
Her face changing into a frown
Molly is the girl
To take you on a twirl
Whoopee cushion on the teacher's seat
In the sweltering summer she's turning up the
heat
For the boys she'll flirt and pull up her skirt
Just like the boys she'll play in the dirt
Climbing high into a tree
Leaving most of her tea
Stealing from the sweet shop
Outrunning the overweight cop
Hopscotch with white chalk
Eating with her knife instead of her fork
Pulling out her tongue
Being cheeky to her Mum
A real rebel, a tomboy at heart
Burst out laughing to the sound of a fart
Causing havoc with the neighbours
Not doing her parents any favours
Giggling away in church
Leaving you in the lurch
Time to play, knock and run
Round the chip shop to fill her tum
Laughing at someone else's expense

Tearing her school uniform climbing over the
fence
A clenched fist at authority
As all the rules and regulations drive her potty
Always involved in cat fights
Sitting in detention most nights
Smoking behind the bike shed
Turning one of her mates faces red
Picking up a handful of ants
Shoving them down another boy's pants
Itching powder down someone's back
A well-placed stone on the railway track
Yeah, Molly, the tomboy of today
Will she ever grow up, who can say?

Outstanding Still

To be again, what once I was
To feel the rush of adrenalin, just because
But now look at me, a shadow of my former self
Weighed down by many years, struck down by
health
A legend to be remembered
My age and time instantly cured
For that split second in time
Make me stand out and forever shine

Rust Bucket

Shiny and bright, clean and new
I think I'm so lucky, one of the few
But slowly I'm punished for being too lazy
And now I'm going out of my mind, turning
crazy
For my once new stylish shiny car
Had me saying "Owwwwwww," but now
"Ahhhhhhhh!"
It's gone from brilliant green to decaying rust
Scratching my head, repair is a must
But it's far too late as the damage is done
I'm now just praying it continues to run
For the engine still purrs and the wheels still turn
So the open road still awaits, money to burn

The Dead Ghost

I really didn't know him that well
But then I don't think anybody did
He was very much a loner
Never married, no family
A bit deaf
I think he said something about being in the war
Strange sense of humour
Used to laugh at the weirdest things
Nobody knew him well
He was a very private person
Liked his independence, his freedom I guess
Lived alone, died alone
Nobody at his funeral, nobody grieving over his
death
Gone forever
But then alive he was a ghost

A Dot in the Distance

I ran and ran up the hill
Away from shattered dreams and a hateful bitter
past
I reach the top and turn to look on her
She is now just a speck on the horizon
A fading memory pricking my subconscious
She's all I had and now I've lost her
It's no good. I can't go on anymore
And where I'm going, she can't come
I will be lost to her forever
But this is way it must be
Heartbreak is such a pain to endure
And I shall grieve for her always
I take one last look at her
A tiny shape across the hills
And I turn away in tears
For now this scene will stay with me
For now she will remain forever in my head
Forever tormenting me
As the dot in the distance

War Kiss

Across the barbed wire our lips meet
Tasting each other, taste so sweet
Our last kiss until the end of the war
Soon be to left gazing at each other's
photographs
Wanting more, so much more
Being pulled back our lips part
And so our hard lonely journey's begin
I hear screaming and anguish too great to
measure
Trying to stay calm, for god's sake
As I turn to see my love marched away
Utter despair drains my body of life
As she disappears away into the oncoming storm
Our love destroyed by war
A war none of us wanted
Who is to answer for this agony?
For we are just another couple of casualties in
just another war

Castle of Sand

Castle of sand
Made by hand
For protection and shelter
On life's helter-skelter

Castle of sand
Stands on my land
For me and my wife
As we await life

Castle of sand
Looking fine and grand
Children to play
Just another day

Castle of sand
To make a stand
Left on my own
All the others flown

Castle of sand
Nobody left in my band
Life's just one lonely day
No hope just pray

Castle of sand
All that I planned
Now it tatters
My end is all that matters

Castle of sand
An end to be found
Nowhere left to hide
Swept away by the tide

Castle of sand
Collapsed land
House of cards
Fallen stars

Arc of the Galaxy

Slowing to impulse 2 to look at the great rift,
where so many a young pilot lost their life.
I close my eyes, and in the depths of the
darkness,
I can hear their screams,
I can see the sparks like glitter,
lightning up the death of a young life for a split
second,
and then nothing.
Oh the fear, and the pleasure,
it still haunts me, it still makes me shudder,
but I am glad to have looked on it for one last
time.
The rift now glows bright green, mingling with
the stars,
and the energy given off by Rycile,
the outer planet that was obliterated.
It's still out of bounds for all space traffic,
and will remain so for another 2 life-spans.
I blast off into light speed and go into cryo sleep.

"BEEP! BEEP! BEEP! - COULDRON
SYSTEM APPROCHING!"
My ships computer system wakes me.
I rise and splash some water on my hot sweaty
face,
and walk through the corridors to the main
cockpit and sit.
I press the conductor accelerator, and watch the

stars become long lines,
that I now become part of.
The Couldron system holds another bundle of
memories for me,
my worst nightmare, which will soon be over.
I steer the ship towards the great planet Rymon.
It appears through my left window,
round and quiet, sitting happily in its
contentment of time.
I warp towards it wondering how the decaying
south eastern segment has fared since the war,
through the ages.
My ship slides along through the vastness of the
galaxy with ease,
as I come up on Rymon.
It looks bad, god it's bad.
The small grey planet is still devouring itself,
its disease getting much worse.
I fly up closer to observe the wound it received,
way back in the first time of light,
received by me!
The guilt now destroying me like a cancer.
The whole lower south easterly section of the
planet is a blaze with fire,
huge meteors constantly come away from the
planets crust,
gliding away into space,
as the planet slowly tears itself apart,
dying in agony, leaving a sickly yellow glow
blazing through the heavens,
and now stabbing at my conscious, making me

weaker with every breath.
Looking deeper into the decaying crust I see
bright searing white liquid,
once the essence of the planet; the building
blocks of life itself.
What an end! What shame!
The guilt mine, but not for much longer.

I walk to the hanger bay, and open the outer
doors;
the package I prepared is released, and goes. (I
hope.)
To my children, bless them.
I walk back to the cockpit and throttle up into a
collision course with Rymon.
I sip some water and sit and wait for impact.
Spying the fire planet,
Long since burned, and soon my body shall join
it,
and my guilt.
In a sudden attack of rage and guilt I try to make
the craft go faster,
trying the afterburners that I know won't work,
they have long since been silent,
hit by a laser blast by the sector police.
I escaped them, but maybe it would have been
better if they had caught me,
executed me for genocide,
but I had to run, if only for my family, my
children.
They got my wife and executed her, but not my

children,
poor Emma....
Well they shall not have me. I shall rule my own
ending.
No noose around my neck, no laser blast in my
chest.

The craft hurtles towards the decaying blazing
planet,
Rymon with devastating speed.
I begin to feel the warmth of the endless fire,
my endless fire that I started all those light years
ago,
the endless fire that has engulfed the ashes of a
trillion souls,
and now the one responsible for the trillion, shall
end his suffering.
All inside my cockpit alarms are going off and
the ships computer won't shut up!
"WARNING! WARNING! WARNING!
PLANET COLLISION IMMINATE!
WARNING! WARNING!"
I knell on the floor and stare at my looming
doom, and my looming release,
as my craft hurtles out of control into the mouth
of the searing fire,
to be free of the weight of my conscious.

At last.
The craft now shakes and quivers as it shoots
towards the white crust at lightning speed,

34

now melting under the intense heat and breaking
up.
I see a huge fire, a huge red fire. I am a red fire.
RED,
burning heat, I AM FIRE. A.........

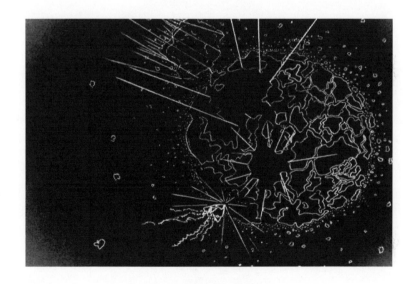

Going Back to Yesterdays

Summer and winter that has gone
Snow and ice that flower long
Fond memories that will never fade
Lazily lying in the spring glade
The heat of the mist, the chill of the sun
Dreaming of the promise of what is still to come
Yet the wind blows full circle and the starts
shine bright
Rising high in the heavens, everlasting light

My Angel in Heaven

Swing, swing on your swing
Glide, glide through the air
Like an angel from heaven
Pure, a spirit of loveliness.

Dry, dry your tears
Cry, cry like waves
That rush down from your eyes
That roll down your cheeks.

Come, come into my arms
Feel, feel the beating of my heart
And we shall never be apart
Locked in the embrace of love.

Float, float away
Blend, blend into the night
Search your feelings, touch your soul
And wake to a new dawn, burning bright.

Away, away night did go
Lost, lost to my sight
A light to guide me, a path to show
Through the day that meets the night.

Fairies, fairies take me high
Higher, higher to the place
To look on her with mine eye
Touch her skin, stroke her face.

Awake, awake from this dream
Child, child talk your speak
Give me knowledge to know what you mean
Yonder is heaven, to wise and meek.

Pray, pray for your life
Weep, weep the fairest is slain
Never now to be my wife
In my arms I carry you away.

Rest, rest in the garden of peace
Torn, torn, I'm a broken man
Long shall I morn your scent, your smell, your
gentle hand
Soon I will join you, to be reunited beyond the
confines of this land.

Die, die to enter heavens magic spell
Rejoice, rejoice as we two that were lost, are
now found
Let our souls become one, forever be bound
To dance, dance for eternity, for we are loves
eternal boy and girl.

The Cornish Walk

Along the path, over the land
Walking together, hand in hand
Silent dead tin mines surround by a barbed wire
cage
Reminders to us all of a by – gone age
Seagulls wail, seagulls cry
Far out to sea, high in the sky
The path is long, twist and turn
Weather beaten over centuries, freeze and burn
Sweltering sun, fine misty rain
Covering the land, picturesque and plain
Fertile green land, wild swaying flowers
Ancient granite cliff, age–long it towers
A small harbour town
Where granite did once topple down
Our costal path walk
Picnic walk and talk.

Scorched Oil

Thick brown scorched oil
Left in the desert to bake and boil
Hard road of sand, wind of dust
Burnt to a cinder, cooked into crust
Drip from an engine, sweat from a hand
Where is the water in this god – forsaken land?
140 degrees, every day by noon
For any exposed, life is just a burning doom
Left to rot in a furnace of fire
The desert of death, funeral pyre.

Bridges Over Rivers

Water flowing
Always trying to get somewhere else
Never happy where it is
Just like people
Constantly moving around
Always wanting to be somewhere else
And when they get there
There off again
To somewhere else
Only to move off yet again
Never happy, never content
The entire population of this planet
Travelling somewhere
Like an out of control train
Be somewhere else
By run or by walk
By wheel or by rail
By air or by talk
By wing or by rail
Bridges over rivers
Bridges over bridges
Bridges over gridlock
Gridlock over gridlock.

The Rape of the Landscape

This is the place where once grass did grow
This is the place where once wildlife did live
Rising concrete jungle, brick seeds to sow
Extinct legacy, left to give.

A sea of blue where fishermen do toil
A vast sea, rich with beauty and fish
Destroyed and polluted with thick brown
clinging oil
Reversal of ecological disaster, just a wish.

Getting too cold, migrate south
Feather that fly, follow the sun
Understanding their pattern, word of mouth
Nature reserve in sight, if make it past the gun.

To live, to breathe, to drink and feed
Why does man make our earth bleed?
For every living creature and plant in need
For man's ignorance, fear and greed.

Where do the Experts go?

Where do the experts go?
They must go somewhere?
Who does the dentist see for his toothache?
Who takes away the dustman's rubbish?
Who does the doctor see when they are unwell?
Who bakes for the baker?
Who does the DJ listen to?
Who teaches the teacher?
Who does the policeman call when he's
burgled?
Which airline does the pilot fly with?
Who fixes the mechanics car?
Who does the sailor cruise with?
Which bus does the bus driver catch?
Who nurses the nurse?
Who does the vet choose to tend his sick pet?
Where does the holiday rep go to on holiday?
Whose meat does the butcher buy?
Whose books does the author read?
What music does the musician listen to?
Who makes the comedian laugh?
What films does the director watch?
What does the TV star watch on TV?
Who fixes the builders house?
What paper does the editor read?
What car does the car maker drive?
They are the experts
But who do they choose?

The Sun Before the Dawn

Lost, forever in the dark
Who will help me now?
Hating this world, the dogs bark
To them, I shall never bow

But there she is, guiding me into the light
Silhouetted against the silver moon
Giving me heart and strength for the final fight
Now for the end, to be back with her soon

Now confronted them, time to face my fear
Their attacks bounce off me, for now I have her
strength
So I make them listen, and all becomes clear
Power surges inside me, any height, any
distance, any length

Crushed by my hand, victory is mine
I collapse at her feet, calm after the storm
To me she is everything, in darkness she will
always shine
She, the life in my body, the sun before the dawn

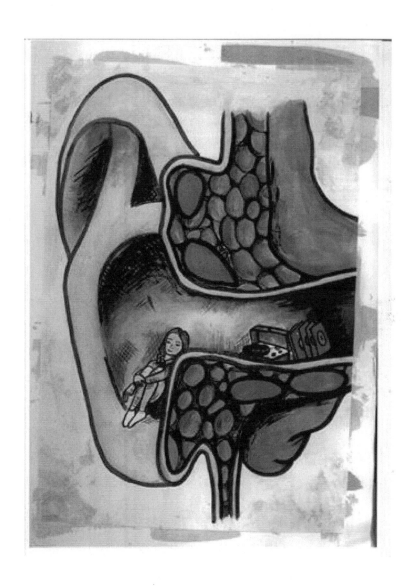

Interceptor Star

There it is, the interceptor star
What a magnificent ship, it's huge
Look at all those windows, thousands of them
All gazing out to space
Soon we'll be docking and we will be home
At last, away from earth
Earth; just left to decay, slowly decay
After our hosts destroyed it
Left it a blazing poisonous rock
Still they had no choice, did they?

Man-made war inevitable
Man and war are partners
Man seems to feel more comfortable with war
Than giving the unknown a chance
Anyway I wonder what our new life has in store
for us.
I wonder what our rooms will be like.
I hope we make friends
I wonder if any of our old friends from earth
made it
Maybe we'll see them on board

Our shuttle is now right up to the interceptor
stars hull
There's the docking hold, lights flashing all
around it
That's odd; I thought I just saw one of those
mutants!

I'm sure it just appeared at that window!
No, it can't be… I don't feel good about this
Ah, here we go, docking now
Oh don't worry kids they'll take care of us
Won't they?
The computer speaks 'Docking complete.'
Doors open

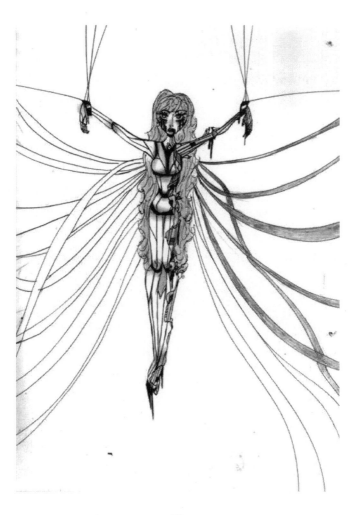

Everything and Nothing and Something

In-between

In my many moments
I seek the perfect one
From my waking eye
Until the day is done

Looking for a lifetime
Above and below land
Longing to finally meet you
And shake you by the hand

Why do I carry this burden?
A self-inflicted wound
Cast ashore on my desert island
Forever alone, marooned

In the hours of darkness
I see her in my sleep
From this dream may I never wake?
For all my tomorrows can keep

This is some light I see
A unique being for me
Today we'll dance in melody
Joining me, to be

But the dream turns to nightmare
As I wake for another day

Once more down the endless road
To crossroads that point another way

My hopes seemed dashed
Many people help, and hinder
Always searching for this one
Through spring, summer, autumn and winter

Head in my hands
Glad to be back
Failed and exhausted
Off the endless rising track

Now life's acceptable
Live for the day
Each one as it comes
It's the only way

Whatever will be, will be
She'll come when she comes
I'll leave the searching to her
Under many moons and suns

But I have not given up hope
In finding my one perfect girl
But whatever, I know one day it'll end
In everything or nothing or something in-
between

Forgotten Stories Never Told

Before the big bang there was nothing
After the sun goes supernova the will be nothing
All those people, all those animals
All those flowers, all those trees
All those achievements all the atrocities
Everyone has their own personal stories
Through their journey of life
A trillion stories
Lost in a single breath
Lost in a single blast wave
Forever silenced
Forever silence

Dark Shadow

Slowly stirring in the corner
Just out of sight
Quiet, tentative, almost
Creeping nearer
Creeping across the carpet
Seizing you with a terror
A shiver down your body
Dark shapes
Shapes that frighten you subconscious
Going bump in the night
Hiding under the covers
Dark shadows lurking
Waiting to pounce
A paralyzing sight
Of dark shadows

Ballet of the Sunset Angel

Act1.

She dwelt for the years of her youth
blessed and dancing in the fields and valleys on
the farm
loved and cared for by her mother and father
innocent face of youth, mischief, and wonder
she grows into a slender teenager
ever the stares of male eyes from near and afar
she teases them with her playful spirit.

Slowly the years pass, and what was once young
and cute; pupil
is now adult, and beautiful: butterfly
flower opened by the spring sun
her body slim and curved
her hair light brown and tied back
a few hairs curl round the side of her face
her graceful nature, the envy of every woman in
the county
and yet, she is no threat
she stays loyal to her parents and the farm
working and playing with the animals
a picture of happiness, their daughter, sent from
heaven.

Gathering hay in the heat of the summer
rejecting advances from the bare chested local
muscles

she's waiting for that one special dark stranger
someone who has no past, no rumors, no
baggage
and so she dreams, daydreams, on the haystacks
and a handful of hay is thrown over her by her
father
she falls back laughing, brushing the hay away
chasing her father, laughing
the dark stranger, for now forgotten.

That night she dreamed, and there he was
she could not see his face, he had no face
for he was the face that would be
he holds her tight in his arms
and they both dance, together they dance in the
dark forest
sending the creatures of the night scurrying for
cover
the bats flapping away towards the moon
through the heavens and back again, they danced
into waterfalls and over mountains, through
rainbows
sprinting back and fourth into new dimensions
of joy
she tossed and turned, happy to be with him
him, him, who was he? Where was he?
When would he come to her? How long must
she wait? When?
The sound of the cock's crow wakes her,
opening eyes
morning has dawned; now he dances alone, until

tonight
morning has dawned.
When?

A loud knock on the farm door
she opens it to see.... A stranger to these parts-
but wait...him... Is it him?
Come to her, could it be? At last?
He is tall with black hair.
He looks strong, and is very handsome
he is new to the area and is looking for work
she beckons him to enter and goes in search of
her father
running, pulling her father back to the farm
house
with her head filled with his handsome face
filled with a light heart, filled with love.

Staring at him from her bedroom window
not able to get his face out of her thoughts
she goes to him while he works bailing hay, she
helps him
how strong he is, how fresh he looks, a new
perfect man
in a county filled with ordinary.
The two sit and chat, her eyes sparkle
the glint of the sunshine catches her white teeth
he takes in her beauty, her fragrance, her curves
so many curves, and so many hidden behind the
soft prison called material.

The days pass, and the two get closer
from his door farmer and wife observe the two
in the fields
holding hands they dance round and round and
collapse on the ground
her parents laugh and go back into their farm
house happy for their daughter.
The two lovers gaze at each other
he rolls over and kisses her deeply with passion
a kiss that she will remember forever
lips tightly pressed together, bursting with
mingling juices
twisting tongues tied in a knot, the soft touch of
skin
she's in heaven again, but this time she is not
dreaming
a face is on this man, the man in her dream.
He is in heaven
heaven rejoices in a parade of joy
colour's explode in splendor, and the whole
place shakes
for love is the greatest power,
and as evening draws on, the two sit and touch,
taste and feel, and listen
birds twittering, singing their songs of love to
the two
happiness is in both their hearts
as the sun goes down blood red in the heavens.

Act 2.

Him and her, gossip spreads like wild-fire
the two detected from the norm
living a secret life of love alone on the farm
togetherness, feelings of love flutter between the
two
a match made in heaven, how can this dream
end?
As the weeks flow into months
so much love, so happy, so lucky
a prayer for the two, kneeling, looking up at
Jesus
"Oh dear lord, thank you for him, thank you for
her. Amen."
Outside, the sky darkens.

A letter delivered in haste, a worried concerned
look
packing in a hurry, he must get away today
back to his sick mother, before it's too late
a horse laden down, galloping away from the
farm
the two come to the lane
a hand gripping hand, a cuddle, a kiss
a tear wiped away,
vows spoken, a promise, promised
galloping away, a wave
a lonely walk back
how different everything looks when events take
a turn for the worst.

She sits on the fence, legs dangling and
swinging
she hears his last words to her echo round in her
head.
"I'll return to you soon, my love."

Kneeling, hand held out full of corn
the pecking of hungry beaks
the quaking of ducks, splashing in the pond
the grazing of cows, in lush green field's
oh, the torment of lost love
why now? Why no word? What's happening?
Why has he failed to send word?
Watched by her parents, she plods around the
farm and fields
hands thrust deep in her skirt pockets
depressed and heart-broken
with her head full of a thousand unanswered
questions
her sparkle and graceful nature gone
darkened by an evil spell
which only one man has the power to deliver her
from
but he is far, far away.

Months pass, she all but lost her graceful spirit
days of agony roll into another
how once a fair maiden, happy and radiant
has changed into a living breathing ghost, sad
and alone
tied down by her feelings of what was

what could have been, dashed forever
hidden tears shed, frozen into a cold hard edge
an attitude never before seen
her shame in the eyes of gossip
gossip-mongers of spite
tearing out her hair with questions, until he
returns to her dreams
the stranger with no face is back
the stranger of her dreams, has returned.

A winding path, curling its way up to the cliffs
clusters of wild flowers, and the busy bumble
bees
a fresh cool wind, a sunny warm day
the wailing of the gulls, the crash and boom of
the waves
breaking and battering the age old rocks
the view, stretching for miles and miles.
She wanders in a daze, a changed person
a sad face, but still a beautiful face
waiting for something to happen.

She walks and walks, stumbling and plodding
along the coastal path
and there, growing by the edge of a rock
she spies some hay weed.
How her mother and father would love to see
some hay weed
and brew it for tonight's supper.
Carefully she lowers herself down between the
rocks

she picks the flower
but a sudden gust of wind blows her cream skirt
up
she panics, and loses her footing and grip
she slides and rolls down the steep grassy slope
stopping right on the cliffs edge.
She looks down and goes dizzy in the head
she inches forward from death, as the wind
increases in strength
tossing her skirt and hair in all directions
seized by terror, she cannot move
her black stockinged legs dangle over the edge
how peaceful the coast remains, its beauty
disguising its danger
unaware of her plight and unforgiving
she calls out, with her soft pitiful cry
clinging onto the bank, her life hanging by a
thread
and in this spit second she sees how foolish
she's been
there's more to life than a broken heart
and time is the healer
if only she had more time
and now across the sea, comes the sunset.
The crunch of gravel, a step nearer
a hearing of a damsel in distress
a walk turned into a run
skidding at the paths edge, to the rescue
he carefully makes his way down
light feelings blossom in her heart
another stranger, another handsome stranger.

Act 3.

"Don't be frightened, hold on tight, and don't
look down."
Closing her eyes, holding onto him
he lifts her out of her plight
yet an unseen new plight is born.
She is overcome with grief
and giving him directions back to the farm
she faints
her beautiful frail body is in his arms
and he walks towards the farm.

A frantic mother, a worried father
a cool flannel placed on a hot forehead
and open eyes, deep beautiful brown eyes
explaining her story, and no hay weed to show!
But relief flows from all, for her life is their life
a pat on his back, a meal, and new friends
the stranger looks down on his new friend
she lies in her bed, tired and weak
strengthened by his touch
and to hear his voice
her heart is filled with warmth
and his words that he will see her, tomorrow.

A guarded renewal, she could not bare another
betrayal
but her emotions run high, and her hormones are
calling out
for a face, to the stranger of her dreams

in her mind she looks back on his face, and body
tall, muscular, broad-shouldered and strong
brown hair and sweet brown eyes
that night her dream returned
and they danced again in the woods above the
world
and the man had the face of her rescuer.

The next day he returns as promised, and her
feelings of happiness
and her feelings of joy are united as one.
Slowly a bond is tied between the two
the handsome man from the next county, and the
farmer's daughter
a romance blossoms between the two
love is only a matter of time
a renewed radiant glow, shimmers all around her
flowing from her, bringing back to the world her
former self
she is happy and full, in spirit and the joys of life
dancing through the grassy meadows, picking
wild flowers
talking to the animals
and over the horizon he comes to her
and she runs to him, embracing and momentarily
lost in a world of tightly pressed bodies and lips
pick nick in the woods, with the wildlife and its
secrets.

Hanging up the washing, what a tedious job
but wait, there he is, coming over the brow of

the hill
with the sunset at his back,
quickly she finishes hanging out the washing
and drops the peg-bag
running inside to tell her parents
quickly she fusses with her hair and frock
running out of the farmhouse, scattering the
chickens.
Over the gate and through the fields, full of
mooing cows
over the style, and up the lane to meet him
drawing nearer and nearer
but wait.....That's not right...something's wrong
it's not him
oh my goodness, its, it's not him, it's the other
man
returned from his sick mother!!!
Oh NO!!!!!
Her heart melts, and burns inside her, ignited by
guilt
the guilt of her false smile to greet his smile
and the guilt of her broken promise, that stabs at
her soul
as worry grips her rigid.

Act 4.

A drop of heavy bags, run and cuddle
kissing and holding tightly, she courses through
his veins
confusion racks her brain, she pulls away
smiling and happy, and his reasons for being
away so long???
Travel to exotic locations with family
after the death of his mother, just to get away,
comfort his sister
but now, new and invigorated, he's back
back to claim his prize, and is staying in the
nearby inn
promises of tomorrow, confusion
utter confusion.

That night the dream was horrible
the man was back, hand in hand they danced
again in the woods
but his face, his face is a muddled mixture of the
two
melting and twisting into a sick mask of evil.
She wakes in a start, wiping the sweat from her
brow
what to do? How to keep to two apart? What to
do?

The second is first, asking to walk the cliffs
she declines, work to tend to....the first lie!
He will stay and help her, and now life turns to

conflict
the first is second, two cocks, strutting their
spurs
"Who is he?" Explain?
She can't answer
she falls to the ground, clasping her ears,
shaking her head
her long hair flowing into a beautiful desperate
tangle
looking up at her two men
rescued by her father, the men told to leave
inside she reaches the depths of her soul, and
there she is trapped.

The two hold a council and demand her to
choose one
she comes to them, and looks with tearful eyes
a desperate face, red and swollen from the agony
of loves tears
both so much her life, both so special, both part
of her
she gives no answer, and is helped back in,
dragging legs
the two hold a council of war, and go to the
gunsmith
the referee will take them in the morning
to preside over another.
Pistols at dawn!

The referee sends word to the farmhouse, as per
instructed by the two

she goes out of her mind
the doctors drugs help her, to help her sleep
but the dream is so vivid
he is there, but she is not
he is looking for her, but he finds her not
and slowly he fades away into the distance,
walking away forever
and in the dead of dawn, she wakes
quickly she dresses, and dashes out of the
farmhouse
over the gate to the stable
onto horse, and far away.

It's a cold crisp summer morning, the larks fly
over the trees
and pass over the men who are assembled
in the long wide field, shrouded in early morning
mist
beside a huge oval lake
a coffin is lowered from the horse-cart
another is on the cart.

Both men remove their jackets
and each chooses a pistol
the referee talks to both and both shake hands.
They stand back to back
both see her in their hearts
for the prize of her beauty is worth the duel
worth dying for
failure is not comprehendible
and death is better than rejection

70

neither could now live, not without her.

The horse jumps the fence, and comes through
the woods
she jumps from her mount, and runs up to the
hedge
looking on the field
her men, her two men
and their striding away from each other
both wearing long white shirts, each holding a
pistol
a man stands to the side of them, counting
numbers
"Six, Seven, Eight, Nine, TEN!"
She shudders, her heart skips a beat.
"STOP. THIS MUST STOP NOW!"
She climbs the hedge and runs with all her might
towards them
a sight of wonder and beauty
like a stricken ghost,
her long white skirt, clumsily, flowing and
sticking to her long slim legs
sapping her strength, and slowing her progress
and tiring her arms
her hair in full-flow, beautiful in her female
being.
"ELEVEN, TWELVE, THIRTEEN,
FOURTEEN,"
past the cart and the coffins, "FIFTEEN,
SIXTEEN, SEVENTEEN,"
past the referee, "EIGHTEEN, NINETEEN,"

71

she slides to a stop in-between her two lovers
holding up her arms
"Please stop this." she whispers in her attempt to
speak.
"TWENTY!"
They don't hear her and both turn and shoot!
Both bullets hit her; she falls to the grass, dying.

Act 5.

Her men and the others gathered run to her
her fist cradles her head.
"Speak to me love."
"Oh goodness, what have we done?"
She cries tears, a tear for pain, a tear for failure,
a tear for her parents
a tear for the farm, a tear for memories, a tear for
her life
a tear for her death, a tear for her two lovers
a tear for wasted love, a tear for the torment of
love
a tear for.....LOVE.
And yet the love in her dying heart and soul is so
powerful,
it now prepares for the afterlife.

The two men grieve over her body
slowly floating away
as the blood of her life stains her white dress
leaking away her life
she dies, with a crying scream of love
to love man, not to be, only to love man.
The coffin is hammered shut
and the little pony trundles off, carrying her to
heaven.

Carried to the church, by the two
whose sentence is a life of endless grieving
for taking the life of the sunset angel

her parents wholly overcome with grief, and
desperation
the coffin lowered in, and a shot of gravel and
mud tossed in.

Unseen she rises in glorious display of beauty
as the sun breaks through the cloud
shinning down on her coffin, she's flying above
them all
shimmering in the power of god
lit up as an angel, as the doors of heaven open
for her
and she looks down for one last time on her
loves and her parents, and her farm
so many happy memories
and with the turn of her head, she fly's towards
god
greeted by other angels, who swirl all around her
and then they leave her a trail to the gods front
gate to follow
and she flies through the trial, and the blinding
light of god
and she flies up and up and up through the gate
to live for an eternity in love, for love
for she was, and always will be, LOVE.

Lost Forever

I can still remember
How we used to be
Feeling each other
Always together
In you I see me

Hand in hand we travelled
Face to face we talked
In the magic of love
Cast from above
This earth on which we walked

I still love you so
You'll always be mine
Lost forever
In a moment
For a life time

Lost forever
Ever searching
On this planet
For your face

In the darkness of separation
I still hear your voice
Day after day
Released from your lips
Your secret song, my choice

I still smell your perfume
Lingering in rooms
Now it's my savior
Mine to savor
Drawing me nearer
I'll be with you soon

I still adore you so
Your spirit stirs in me

Lost forever
Slipped away
Through my fingers
For all time

Lost forever
Hidden from me
Forbidden fruit
Taste so sweet

So I draw towards you
My journey at an end
Standing before me
Looking so lonely
Just like in my dreams

I reach out to touch you
You fade away

Lost forever
My sweet angel
Far away
From my eyes

Lost forever
For tomorrows
From yesterdays
For all days

Lost forever
Gone for good
Final journey
Without me

Lost forever
I'll keep on searching
Never give up
To the end of my days

Super-fortress Obliterator

Our hungry dawn
History's forever day
By night one side would burn
The other cheer and sway

Engines ignite, smokes roar
Sliding down an endless runway
Soaring high
Angel of death

High in the sky did she roar
Devastating cry of rage
Stop to listen, staring at the sky
See the terror, scream, and panic, flee

Open bay doors
Dropping pay load
Lines and lines of pay load
On and on and on and on

A truce a lie
Nowhere to run
Funeral pyre
Tainted earth

Red inferno
Super-fortress obliterator
A once green and fertile land
Wither, crackling, dust

Rays of sun glint on mighty metal
Monster returns back to its cave
Debrief
Turn off the lights

Rocket Away

You're all the same, day in day out
All getting on each other's nerves, driving me
crazy
Why can't you all just leave me alone?
Can't you understand I need my own space?
But NO, you continue to force yourselves on me
Trespassing on my privacy
Making my life hell

You're all so predictable
Driving your cars, going to work
Cheating and deceiving, shouting and screaming
From the neighbors over the fence to the
gridlock on the road
Fighting wars with no cause
Bitching and moaning day and night

Mad men over the sea, saying it to the streets
Is there no space left to me
This overcrowded world just pushed me over the
edge
The constant everyday finally ground me to
breaking point
Am I the only one?

So I retire to my dream, and I climb into my
rocket
I strap myself in and press the button
I feel the engines ignite and the power under me

Then I feel the thrust of fire and release
Oh what a release
To rocket away from you all
As the fireworks go off in my head
The framework holding the rocket disintegrates
Under the intense heat, crumbling ablaze
My rocket blasts up into the sky
Searing speed out of the earth's atmosphere
Into space
Dark, desolate, empty, quiet, space

At last, alone
As I make my way to my new home
I look out of the round window looking back
down at earth
Now so small and getting smaller as my rocket
powers away
And as for the earth
You can have it
You people who ruined it
As I come to my self-made solitude
At last, alone, peace, quite

But I end with an uneasy thought
How long do I have until you all discover this
place?
How long do I have until I am invaded?
Even this far away
My haven of peace and quiet

LET THE FRONTIER GROW

The Hero's Heroine

Dark times melody
Ancient fires roar
Mystical powers tragedy
End in deaths red gore

Behold the truth speaker
A hero's quest awaits
Behind a veil ever bleaker
Evil never abates

A wondrous child
So cute, so fair
Her sweet ways, eyes wild
Kneels to say her prayer

Evils wrath, bringer of war
Killing and pillage, for evil glee
Never forget what we saw
Her eyes turn vengeful piercing all to see

She stands alone upon the hill
Spying the cruel army on the run
Not one more shall they kill
Now an end to this horror, their fun

Illuminated in the dark
Fire lights the sky
On each she makes her mark
As the evil ponder how and why

85

The wind howls, blowing her hair and dress
The evil army routed by a shuddering force
Torn apart by her magic powers, how? He can
only guess
Now let nature take its course

Exhausted by the magic she falls
Together they travel back to her home
Guided by rejoicing calls
For time now on, we have never known

The hero and his heroine talked about for years
Never seen again, quietly slip away
Through many generations and many downed
beers
She to disappear forever in the opposite way

Who was she? What was she?
He never knew to his dying day
Who was he? For he will always remain dear to
me
For only the legends can say

Supermodel Blues

The only way to be a winner
Is to be thinner
Thinner, thinner and more thinner
Thinner than any of the other girls
Barely weighing more than a crumb
If that is what it takes to make you number one?
Showing off some fancy freaky designers over
the top clothes
Down all the famous catwalks in all the over
hyped shows
Vogue, cosmopolitan, vanity fair
All much of a muchness, couldn't really care
Catfights in the wardrobe, a ladder in her tights
Outfits no one will ever wear, sore eyes seeing
the sights
After a hard days modelling she rests her weary
head
But she can't ignore her stomachs protests
'YOU HAVENT FED!'
Fingers down her throat, regurgitating down the
loo
Empty plate on the table, one calorie or two?

89

Once Upon a Dream

For everyone who dreams.

The swirling dawn mist calls out to me on the very edge of a dream, I awake for they are calling out to me from the other side and to them I go with glee in my heart. The mist parts, guiding me into the secret garden and taking a quick glance back to my fading house. I open the gate and walk through into wonderland.

There they are again; still sitting at the table I see Alice, The Mad Hatter, and the Cheshire Cat.

They beckon me to join them for tea and cakes. I sit next to the mad hatter who pours me some tea as I take a cake with a cherry on the top. The Queen walks by.

"She's looking for the King." Alice whispers to me.

"Why's that?" I ask Alice. "Well today is their wedding anniversary and I think the King's forgotten." She replies.

The Cheshire cat starts laughing as the mad hatter throws some cake at the Cheshire cat." Touchy subject." He says.

As the Queen walks off Alice shows me her new shoes. Meanwhile the mad hatter and the Cheshire cat trade childish insults about each other. "They are very bright and very red Alice" I say as I sip some tea. "They are going to be for my dancing. Watch me." And with that Alice slides off her chair and begins to gracefully twirl around in her new shoes.

Oblivious the Mad hatter and Cheshire cat now throw cake at each other.

I eat my cake and drink my tea. Alice curtsies and invites me to dance. I take her hand and soon we are both twisting and turning while the white rabbit plays his recorder. The mad hatter and the Cheshire cat copy us and both dance around while cake and tea go flying in all directions. Refreshed I say my goodbyes and promise to return soon. I start to walk away when some way off in the distance I hear the Queen shout with frustration, "OFF WITH HIS HEAD!" Quickly I run down a path that Alice points to as she and the white rabbit stand in front of the path so that the Queen cannot find me. I walk and walk along old lane that slowly widens with trees and then the land in front of me drops so that in the distance I can see a small village. The village seems to be built into the side of the hill. Why it must be Hobbiton.

I walk up to the first cottage to see Bilbo smoking his pipe outside Bag End. I see his large hairy feet and curling smoke coming out of his pipe. He is wearing a green jacket and brown trousers.

Up the road I hear a loud bang and fireworks sparkling over my head. It's Gandalf showing off his latest fireworks to some hobbit children. At the blast from the fireworks Bilbo suddenly jumps up from his midday slumber. "Can't stop," says Bilbo, "got to finish packing for my next adventure." I ask him where he's off to next in middle earth. He looks at me and points over the fields, "Why there, and back again my dear sir." And with that he bounds back into bag end to finish packing. In the distance I can still hear the popping and banging from fireworks. I walk past a row of hobbit cottages and down the lane past a lake.

I carry on and looking to my left I follow a path which goes over a slight hill and down to a house.

As I near it I see a huge beanstalk reaching up

past the clouds. Someone is climbing up it....Its Jack!

I reach the bottom and some impulse inside of me makes me climb it. At the very top, looking down is the face of the giant." Fee Fi Fooo Fum." he booms at the top of his voice, waving to me. I see a goose and around about it a lot of golden eggs. "Mmm don't get any ideas young sir," be booms at me. "That's my golden goose; go find your own if you don't mind. And no before you ask, they are not for sale." I climb up to the top and once again see inside the clouds.

What a spectacular view. The giant then picks me up and says," Where to this time lad?" I look around and point to an area I have not ventured to before. He then hands me a giant dandelion. "Okay, here we go." he booms, and he blows me off the palm of his hand.

I glide through the clouds over mountains and lakes using the giant dandelion to slow down my decent until I descend sharply with a SPLASH, into a river near a wood.

The river winds its way along merrily until I see Rat who's rowing along in his little boat. "AHOY THERE MATEY." he shouts to me. "I'm off to Moles to help him with his latest tunnel extension. Up you get and dry yourself off while I we have a spot of lunch." While I dry my clothes and we glide effortlessly down the river he takes out of a box next to him a red and green picnic blanket and lots of sandwiches and cakes. We are about to begin the feast when Badger calls from the riverbank. "Ratty. Come on we are already late!" Rat quickly packs everything back into his box and steers his little rowing boat next to the bank so I can jump out. "Sorry old chap but we shall have lunch next time when Badgers busy somewhere else. Happy walking."

I watch him row along until he catches up with Badger who's waving at me from across the other side of the river.

I climb out of the river and cross an old wooden bridge to find in front of me a yellow brick road. I see it going off far into the distance and decide to follow.

I follow it past the river and on through many fields and hills. Just as I am feeling tired I stop hearing someone shouting. "HELP! HELP! PLEASE SOMEBODY HELP ME!"

I climb up the yellow path to a low ridge to see far off in a field a man in some distress. I duck under the fence and quickly run towards him. As I get closer I see it's the Scarecrow. "Ohh please help me sir. I seem to have lost my....my...sorry it's very embarrassing. You see I seem to have misplaced my, my, n, n, n........MY NOSE!"

Trying to keep a straight face and not burst out laughing I search the ground and soon find a long carrot.

"Is this it Mr. Scarecrow?" I ask. "Oh Well done young man. What good fortune you came this way for me." I give him the carrot and he quickly places it back in place. "Thank you. Oh that feels much better. Now I can get back to scaring off them damn crows."

I leave him to his scare crowing and soon rejoin the yellow brick road.

I continue to follow it until it runs out just before the start of a wood.

As I get nearer to the wood a witch on her broomstick fly's above me and round and round, cackling to herself. Then in front of me I see Hansel and Gretel. "Ummm, help yourself to the cottage inside the wood," says Hansel." It's yummy." They walk off as I enter the wood.

I follow an old path which to my surprise does

come to a cottage which is made of food. It has a cake roof and ice cream walls, jelly windows and flowers made of icing sugar. I decide to take the door knob which is a biscuit. Very tasty.

A crash in the undergrowth causes me to turn quickly to see Little Red Riding Hood skipping along carrying her basket, followed by three bears. They all dance around and I join in until we all fall over tired.

"Dear me is that the time? I must get to Grandmothers." says Little Red Riding Hood and quickly she's off running back, followed by the three bears.

I carry on and follow the trail for what seems like ages. Suddenly the skies darken and it starts to rain.

The trail leads me to a huge rusty old gate, and beyond I see a tall dark grim looking castle. I am about to turn back when I hear wolves howling nearby. I push the large rusty gates and they squeak open in protest.

I walk up the castle doors as thunder and lightning fill the dark sky.

Frightened I run up to the doors and push them open. SILENCE!

Silence welcomes me as I stand in an impressive vast hall. Corridors go off in every direction. Sinister gothic architecture looms all around at me through archways and corridors. Old statues and paintings seem to stare at me as I make my way tentatively along.

Magnificent embroider tapestries hang from the walls in-between suits of armor, swords and shields.

I come to a large oak door and push it open. I walk in and gasp at the spectacle all round me. The room I now find myself in is a vast library with more books than I have ever seen in my life .

"Bonjour monsieur." Says the candlestick sitting on a large table at the center of the room. "We have been waiting for you." Says the clock sitting next to him.

Suddenly a large roar shakes the entire room. "Ahh I believe the master is waiting for you Monsieur." says the candle stick. "Please follow us." Says the clock.

They guide me along another corridor and down a large winding staircase until I see at the bottom Beauty and the Beast dancing across a beautiful shiny polished floor.

"They have been practicing all day for you monsieur." Entranced, we all look on in awe. Those two are so in love as they glide this way and that in harmony.

When they finish they come over and greet me. Belle kisses my cheek and as she does we all here a clock chime. "Quickly," say's Belle, "Your carriage awaits." She points to some doors to my right.

Without thinking as I hear another chime I run to the doors and throw them open.

As I start to run down the steps I see on one of the steps a single ladies shoe. Another chime breaks my thoughts and I carrying on down the steps to see at the bottom a horse drawn carriage fit for a King and Queen.

I climb in with more chimes echoing in my head. At once the carriage is away as the horses gallop faster and faster through the castle gates, through the wood and beyond into wilderness at awesome speed.

Suddenly as we reach the twelfth chime the carriage comes to a shuddering stop. I climb out and see in wonder that the carriage has turned into a large pumpkin.

Houses are scattered about like we have arrived in a little village, and over the other side of the street there is a huddle of people. There in the centre are Cinderella and the Prince kissing. They smile at me and run past, climbing into the pumpkin. Fireworks explode all around it as it transforms back into a horse drawn carriage.

The horses rear up on their hind legs and in the blink of an eye, it's gone. The people also I notice have all gone. I am all alone. A thick mist engulfs me and a wind parts the mist showing me a pathway. I walk it and soon find myself back in the secret garden and beyond, my home.

I climb back into my warm bed and soon I'm fast asleep.

I wake up with a start, causing several books to fall off my bed onto the floor. I look around and rub my eyes. Then I look down at my books. What an adventure. What wonderful places all my books took me to.

Then I lay back and wait to be taken back. Back into fairytales, back into my dreams.

To the places that live in our hearts, in our dreams where everyone and everything lives happily ever after.

Sunset Blamanche

Inter – setting sun
Red rimmed sky
Pale twinkle of stars
Into a setting sun
Darkens the skies light
Follow your shadow
The cold breath of night
As the host dips under the sea
The candle flame goes out
A trail of smoke
As red turns to black.

Back to the Tramp

The tramp walked along the road
In his torn clothes and worn out shoes
And saw a gypsy ride by
"I wish I were him." Said the tramp
"To have a caravan and a horse to take you
anywhere."

The gypsy travelled along the road
And saw a small run – down cottage
"I wish I lived there," said the gypsy
"To have a warm cottage to live in."

The poor man who lived in the cottage
Looked out of his window and saw the gypsy
caravan go by
Then he looked to his neighbor opposite
"I wish I lived there, "he said
"A much nicer house than my tiny cottage."

The man who lived opposite was on his patio
He looked over his fence to the large detached
house
"I wish I lived there," he said
"Such a lovely house and a much larger garden
than mine.

The busy housewife with two children who lived
there

Looked to the fine stately house on the hill in the distance
"Oh I wish I lived there," she said
"Such open space and peace and quiet, not like this estate!"

The lady who lived in the stately home
Looked to the mansion down in the valley
"What a lucky man." She said
"To own such a fine property. He must be a millionaire?"

The stressed millionaire businessman looked down from his mansion balcony
Worth over a million pounds.
There he saw an old dirty tramp walk by with ripped clothes and battered shoes.
"I wish I were him" said the millionaire
"Look at him, not a care in the world."
"No possessions, no commitments, no letters"
"No repayments, no bills, no worries"
"Free to go where he wants, whenever he wants"
"Not a care in the world. I wish I were him."
He said as he swallowed another headache pill.

Son of the Frantic

I have fought in many battles
In many different forms
With many strange faces
Yet it was always me

My masks litter my mind
Through their slits I've seen all
I've felt all, I've become all
For man can make a difference

Victory and defeat are equal among the dead
For the living taste the sweet and bitter
And I've tasted both
A bitter sweet division to fight for

To command an army
To direct a battle
It lives in your life
How do we sleep and be at peace?

I've been fried in the desert
Frozen in the ice
Covered in the jungle
Bustled in the city

My memories of war
Sit and collect dust
A worthy honour for pride and grace

Only the vanquished enemy, left to face

A pipe from a tribe
A platted tail from horseman
A carpet from the Bedouin
A fish from the artic
A feather from the eagles
A claw from bears
A tooth from a lion
Painted by the aborigines

I only grieve for the dead
Those who died by my hand
Once I thought a man's honour was a battlefield
There's no honour in dying

Never to live again
So many, so young
Never to experience life
Taste of food
Feel of water
Blow of wind
Touch of woman
Elation of joy
Despair in defeat
What a waste
Never to live a life
Make love to a woman
Hold your baby in your arms
Gaze at the stars
Sail on the seas

Soar in the sky
Breathe in life

Honour in battle is at the time
But now I'm haunted by the dead
Only mass crucifixes remain
How many more must die
For the sake of lines on a map?

Medals for killing
Stuffed and displayed over my mantelpiece
I can't look at them now
Not anymore

Once I was a young man
Passionate, wild, frantic
The blood flowed in my veins
I lived for battle, blood and slaughter
I lived for power, stature, and glory
Now that wild son is an old man
There is no wisdom is slaughter
Just endless nights and ghosts
Ghosts that will never leave
This once ignorant, bloodthirsty, power hungry
Son of the frantic

Welcome to the Winter

Burnt dry leaves fall to the wet ground
There's a chill in the air
The evenings are getting darker
The skies are full of cloud
And down comes the rain
And the wind picks up
The temperature drops
There's going to be a covering of frost
So wrap up warm
Be cozy by the fireside
Protected from the freeze
And all that's cold and damp and wet
Prepare to shiver for a few long months
Welcome to the winter

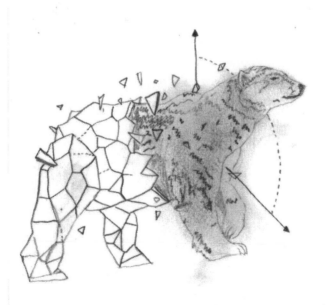

Star Children

An image, a moment
I saw you in the night sky
Displaying your beauty
For us all to see
I felt you're magic
Flowing through me
Travelling through the heavens
Bringing light to dark places
Going to nears and afar
Over the moon, through Venus and past Mars
Children of the night, children of the stars
Looking over us always, from nears and afar

Today and tomorrow, happy and sad
The universe still turns
Time ticks on
The sun brightly burns
When I need help and inspiration, to you I look
Gods star children
Repairing my imperfect life
I pray for your guidance
As I look on you tonight
Blazing across the night sky
Leaving behind your magical trails
Blow wind; blow into your star children's sails
Children of the night, children of the stars
Looking down on us forever, from near and afar

Comrades in Blood

Lost forever in the mud
Lost forever my comrades in blood
Explosions in the distance that we all fear
Became a land to cherish and hold dear

The anniversary comes once a year
I take a step closer to join you near
A hopeful promise for days of peace
For war to end and for war to cease

How I remember the fear and pain
As we all slowly sunk in the mud and the
pouring rain
The hail of bullets, shellshock in the choking fog
As a million young men drowned in hells bog

Now in the sunshine a new time is born
Decades on my comrades I still morn
So I tell my stories as the children's tears flood
As we all remember the horror, and my
comrades in blood

Time is Love

Time is
Too slow for those who wait
Too fast for those who do
Too long for those who hurt
Too short for those who smile
Too quiet for those who party
To loud for those who listen
Too bright for those who hide
Too dark for those who see
But time
For those who love
Is eternal
Day's dawn
Day's darken
The earth turns
Our spirits fly
But love remains
Forever

Moon Desert

Landscape of fine grey dust
Clinging to covered humps and domes and
shapes
Going on and on into the distance
In all directions
Of this eerily silent moon
Footprints remain

Choking on the soot
Gurgling sound shot through space
Blinded by cosmic eclipse
Deafened by silence
Endless darkness
Vaporised tears

Interactive Sleep

Shut eyes
Getting you down
Can't get up
Up and over the high rise
Work and sleep, stop and go
Go with the flow
At the end of energy
Sapped from my body
Pressure cooker
Overload explode
Breakdown sleep
Sleep, a chance to dream
To come back to life

Mondays ... why?

Beyond the Night (Part 1)

Beyond the night
There is day
Where the children endlessly play
Dead to the world
But alive in paradise
Where every day is joyful, happy and nice
The earth's dead children travel through the
night
Pass Venus and its moon
Keep going you'll be there soon
To feel the joy and love, denied on earth
Past Saturn and its huge magical ring
Beyond Mercury and many stars
Ghost on a wing
See them all, little boys and girls
Cute beautiful faces
Long golden curls
Fly now with the angels
Who will guide you to a promised land?
Don't be scared, take my hand
Beyond the confines of this world
Past Valhalla, Hercules and the great bear
To where a great beacon shines so fair
Mighty gates swing open

As you step into forever bliss
Each receiving a warm embrace, and gentle kiss
And never look back
On your torment and pain
For you have been chosen
And you have come
From here your deep wounds will heal
For many healing hands
You will feel
Now gasp at what you see
Come, play for eternity
You and me

In Beauty She Lies

Sad songs rise up from the ashes
Smoke curls up with seeking souls
She whispers through a lifeless heart
Eyes that see a cold world
A spirit lost to life
In beauty she lies
Another innocent statistic
In another bloody war

No rings on her fingers
No beat in her heart
The joy of life taken by a bullet
Her long brown hair tainted with her blood
Touched by no one
No loving warm embrace
Just left to rot in a mass grave

Carried by stretcher
A beautiful young face
A face with no name
Beautiful young life
Gone to the angels
And round her neck a crucifix hangs
A symbol of peace of love
An instrument of terror and pain

A mark of religion and faith
What wars are fought over
What morals die for
What innocents suffer for

Why take her life?
What did she ever do?
The wrong place at the wrong time
War knows no justice or humanity
War sucks all in
Devouring all in its deadly path
Who weeps for her?

How did the sniper feel when he took her life?
Who will remember her?
Who? How? Why? Where? When?
Wars endless questions
Without any hope of answers
Wars deep scars
With me forever
Who will remember this terrible day?
This tragic scene
Her beautiful twisted lifeless dead body
I shall forever

Follow the Passengers

We travel through time
Mystified riddles in rhyme
Mysteries of mine
Take my hands and run with me
Through my dreams
Taking you inside my soul
Never letting go
Push back the barriers
Take the next exit
Crushed with pride
Do you hear that inside?
The beat of your heart
In tandem with mine
With you from the start
Now were at the finish
The ends of the ends
And I'm with you
At the end of the beginning
As we lapse into purity
Console yourself
The next door awaits

What a Beautiful Ugly Wonderful Tragic Lovely Terrible World

Born, a delicate flower
Cast into this world, without say
Leading you down life's pathway
Out of control, your destiny shaped

Dancing through the woods in summer
Lazing in the cornfield, not a care in the world
Over valley and under hill
Winding lane, placid stream
Fine misty rain, hazy summer heat

Mother's sympathy, Fathers help
Backs that bend, hands that mend
The right answer, the final word
A big world, one step away

Worlds away, far away
Evil and greed fester
From the human brain
Greed and money
Is the formula for disaster?

The human body – beautiful
Eyes that shine
Hair that flows
Breasts that curve
Legs that curl

A face that's beauty
Lying dead
Life cut out
Blood flows
Only the end of a life

Run, running forever, young in bliss
In school, with friends
Innocent youth of joy
Freckles on his cheeks
Hair in his eyes
Socks rolled down
Football at all times
Skipping with the girls
Ponytails and plats
Eyes wide and smiles sweet
Child of youth
Spread your joy throughout the world

Turn round, round and down
Turn, turn down and round
Out of the light into dark
Turning round and down
Steeper and steeper
Round and down
Encircling in great spirals of decent
Round and down into darkness

Great black veils glide down
Looking down on chaos
Down and down into evil

Round and down
Down and round, turning and twisting
Round and down, through tranquility
Passing down and round into black

Only evil survives
Laughing mocking sickly grin
Lives lost in decadence
Slaughter in the fields
Billions lost for the lines on a map
Heartless butchers grind their plans
To ruin, for desolation
Round and down, round and down
Round and down, slippery slope
Up on high precipice, down and round to
ruination

Swans glide across the lake
Robins hop over the frost
Rabbits run through the woods
Birds effortlessly fly on the wing
Buttercup shines under her chin
Climb high up the tree
Owls hoot, mice nibble, and spiders weave
Ripped jeans, grazed knees
Eyes deep hidden secrets
Released in a kiss

Fairytale in the garden
Decisions at the crossroads
Fast and furious

To calm and be placid
Years roll by
Mowing the lawn on a lazy summer Sunday
Church bells in the air
Leather on willow
Lunch at the pub

The suffering linked together
Decease and disaster
Now they must answer why
WHY? The root of all evil
Profit and gain, lining ones pocket
Money makes the world go round
And spin out of control
Money makes the assassins flock
And sharpen their knives
Money makes the poor wise
Too late! Far too late!
Money makes the world despise
Building bombs
Monkey makes war
Money makes death
Death makes money
War makes money

A day like no other
Bride and groom
Taking each other forever
Forever against the world

The cracks of time
Innocent youth
The cracks of time
Wise age-long
The cracks of time
Generations of joy
The cracks of time
Generations of misery

When time is over, we are all gone
Who will be smiling? Who will be crying?
Who will be right? Who will be wrong?
Who will be heard? Who will be silent?
What a happy sad double edged song

Cure the hurt and let's finish
However short, however long
Life has its beauty
Life has its danger
Walk with open eyes into tomorrow
The choices are there
For one and all

Broken Castle

Nowhere to run
The end of my fun
Nowhere to hide
Forced to wed a bride
Nowhere to fly
So sit and cry
Nowhere to sing
Removing her ring
Nowhere to walk
Just sit and talk
Nowhere to live
A castle to give
Nowhere to play
Order and say
No one to love
As long as we fit like a glove
Noting to do
But catch the flu
Nothing to make
Except other lands shake
Nowhere to go
End of the show
A kingdom to rule
For a puppet and a fool

Touching the Winter

Today the storm is long away
But it is coming
I can feel it in the air
That warm humid wind
Now turning raw and bitter

The eyes of the sleek fox
The hoot of the clever owl
Hail the coming of winter
Raindrops tap on my window
And everyone's wrapped up in coats

The frost that welcomes you
Good morning time to freeze
Robins hop about in the garden
Water frozen, sap to ice
Cruel and cold

Days turn into weeks
Christmas cheer melts the winter cold
As hearts all over the world embrace
Christmas and the New Year
But winter has the last laugh!

Cows

Cows in a field
Aimlessly wandering
Munching grass and sitting down
While the world goes by, oblivious

Work

I can't have a life
I'm not allowed to enjoy life
I have to work
Morning, afternoon, evening, night
To pay for things
That decay

Aching Joints

Waking up in the dark
For another day
Dull cardboard flakes and milk
Dashing out the door
To join the endless queue
For another dull day at the workface
Same old walls, same old faces
Part of the furniture
Filing paper, writing emails, walking corridors
Digging holes, feeding ravenous machines,
chasing rainbows
Aching joints
As I get ever older
Ever colder

Brick Wall

Today I hit a brick wall
It suddenly just hit me
Why am I here?
What am I doing?
This is not me
This is insane
I can't do this anymore
I want out, now!

I broke through
It hurt
There are scars
I wish I could relax
Enjoy life
Living in constant fear is not good
Nagging at you all the time
Knowing it's not over

Brick by brick
The wall has been rebuilt
I do not want to go through it again
It hurts
It scars
But there it is
Looming

Spec of Light

A gleam in my heart
A longing
Forces pulling towards me
Tide turning
Earth spinning
Light blinding
And there at the very centre
Life

Dragon

Hiding in caves
The one that climbed great heights
The one that once ruled
Striking fear into man
But man is clever
Man is evil
Persecuted and hunted
Always fleeing
Always fearful
Another civilisation
Misunderstood, driven to extinction
Never to hear that roar
Never to feel that fire
Just a picture, a thought, a silent reminisce

Dance

To move and breathe
Climb to extremes, for art
To touch the audience
And make them think
As I twist and turn my body
Expression and passion oozing from every fibre
At one with the music and the tale
As I glide inside hearts and souls
Hearing applause
As the curtain comes down
I gasp for breath
Knowing I gave my all

Love in May

Love in May
Well what can I say?
When male and female play
Their earth will shake on that day.
Love?
What a word
What meaning
Our existence entire, raised on love
Love of woman
Love of man
Pouring out through eons, love to drown
Love of all things
Love; making me go weak at the knees
Like a tree, swaying in a strong breeze
Effecting each one of us differently
Loves magic spell, yours to cast
So powerful it will never go off, but last and last
Until you finally get your chance
To use your magic, leaving you in a trance.

Swirling heads of innocence
Enter please, ladies and gentlemen
Crowds gather the performance looming
Spotlights swooping, hearts blooming
Curtains open
Words of love through eyes spoken.

Love in May
The only way

Spring dawn day
Happy and gay
It's the time of year
For song and cheer
To lay her head in long green grass
A time to remember in the forever past
But for every light side there is a darkness
looming
So rip out my soul heathen beast
On my heart and soul you now feast
Satisfy your hunger
Power monger
Quench your thirst
For you are not the first
It is not love you deserve
For I still have plenty in reserve
All you shall have is my pity
Such a shame for one so pretty.

Love is not lust
Lust is just a moment of must
A thought, a feeling, a quick stab
A dare, a game, a story to blab
Give me love
To feel like a glove
Worship from above
To release like a dove
Oh, what would I give for love?

My life
A sacrifice worthy of her

To keep safe and well
I will give her my life
But where is this angel?
Far far away from me
Perhaps she never was.

To taste her lips
To feel her tongue
Kneeling, stroking her shapely hips
How so beautiful for one so young
Never want to let go
Letting my feelings and emotions flow
Song of love, hear her moan
Up there high upon her throne
In each other, we need
With each other we breathe
To make another we breed
To be with each other, forever sowing the seed
My feelings of love on this day
And the month. Well it happens to be May.

Love in May
Try to find a way
To make her stay
For another day
To hold in my arms
Sit by her and lay
Swept in by her bountiful charms
Faith in her, which I pray
My heart all of a flutter, sound off emotional
alarms

Our love consumed, sunshine's fine rays
An understanding presence that somehow calms
Still be in love, after many more Mays.

It's written in the eyes
A glance that speaks a thought
Feelings dashed, deigned
Loves a magic that cannot be bought
A price immeasurable
Loves only law
Written down through days of ages
No pinnacle higher, more devastating than war
Parchment and quill, frail crumbling pages.

Fire and water
Son and daughter
Sea and salt
Serpent to halt
Sun and moon
Dark crystal Hume
Boy and girl
Hair fine curl
Iron and steel
Touch and feel
Root and tree
Passion must flee
Sweet and sour
Kneel and cower
Love and hate
Forever to mate.

It's such a surprise to break away from your lies
So many commitments and ties
And it's such a shame to hear those wicked lies
Excuses, double standards, sigh
Who can you trust? Who do you believe?
When you've been beaten into the dust
Spurned by your lover for another.

Ancient craft of beauty
Image of priceless grace
In your eyes I see my face
Speak your whisper without trace
To you, only you, I give my duty.

Troubled lands of fire
You guide me through
Just to dash my hopes
On your rocks of trust
Take another, if you must
As I return to the fire and its crust
My thoughts today
In the month of May.

Love in May
I can only pray
Things will go my way
That I'll find her, one day.
They say there is someone out there for
everyone
So where is she?
Why does she hide?

This is no game, it's about life
Our lives, our hopes, our dreams
Lost, to be found
My ears to the ground
Somebody point me in the right direction….for
god's sake!

I sit in the room alone
Lost in my thoughts
On one subject: a partner
How my heart aches for a companion
Now my heart cries out for someone to love
Someone to care for
Someone to laugh with
Someone to cry with
Someone to join with
Someone to sit with
Someone to love
Someone, if only that someone would become a
name
Am I asking too much?
Doesn't much matter
Nobody wants me
So I sit alone, and think…and slowly rot.

I know that if I could inject someone with my
love
What happiness it would bring
Our hearts would cry out and sing
Dance under moon and stars
Journey together to afar

Sleep in each other's arms
Soothing voices that clams
But it is not
I can only dream
And then wake to reality, my torment.

Feeling out for her in the dark
Grasping thin air
Shadows in the gloom
Blinded by the light
My love, out of sight
Screw my eyes up tight
No way out of my plight
Loves just using me to play
Today in May.

Love in May
Another today
What a day
What can I say?
My dream
My lips touch her lips
Our tongues dance
Our tongues feel
Our tongues entwine
Cause I'm your sacred hero
Now we are staring at the edge
Now we are standing on the edge
Now were in love, in May.

Empty Car Park

Have you ever noticed the madness of an empty
car park?
So many cars fighting over a few elusive spaces
They all charge in and they all honk their horns
As they all come so close and yet so far from
parking their cars
You need real skill these days to survive this
urban warfare
So when they drive into an empty car park
CONFUSION! DISBELIEF! PANIC!
They can't quite take it in
They can't quite believe their eyes
So many spaces to choose from
Too much choice
Instead of parking they drive round and round
Round and round and round and round
And round and round and round and round
Disorientated, disconnected, discontinued

Iron Guzzler

Desert as far as you can see
Yellow heat burning
Shimmering haze cracks
Iron trunk standing tall
Sucking at the sand
Guzzling every microscopic drip
A lonely cactus
To stand the test of time

Eliza Atkins   Anisha Rahman

A Parting of Waves

Once you were my everything my everywhere
My morning, evening and night
You were my very sun and stars that ever
twinkled alive
Then time got in our way
A parting of the waves
You went that way and I went the other
A very distance between us
A void awareness
But under the same sun and moon
Breathing the same air and sands
That once entwined us
Now keep us apart

Make a Difference

If one students goes home at the end of the day
from this school
Happy and content, and a little wiser because I
made a difference
It's because others have made a difference
TOUCH, INSPIRE, CREATE, TEACH
For on this great and epic journey of life that we
are all on
I know that one day I will get there
And I know that one day all of you will get there
Like countless others that will come before us
And like countless others that will come after us
I know that one day we shall all get there
Because someone somewhere cares enough
To make a difference

Lick the Lid of Life

If you actually stop and look and listen and
smell and taste
You will see, you will hear
Things around you
That usually passes you by
In your garden, in a field, in your children
Melting ice cream
Blue ripples of the tide
Raindrops pitter patter
Under rainbows and stars
Hand in hands
Tenderness and warmth and cosy and loved
Open eyes, open ears
Senses all
Lick the lid of life

155

Beyond the Night (Part 2)

The gentle swirls of night
Dripping down like a final curtain
Upon this tattered and tiresome day
Twinkle twinkle all the stars
As one by one all the lights go out
Silence descends
Beyond is the night
Inside safe and warm
Outside lay the night
Menacing, brooding, silent
Keeping dawn far away
Beyond somewhere is light
Beyond the night

Bullies

I sit in the corner
Walls closing in all around me
I want the ground to swallow me whole
I never want to leave this room

Why do they pick on me?
Why do they hate me?
What did I ever do to them?
What did I ever do to anyone?

Looking around the empty room
Trying to find a way out
Every way of escape is blocked
As I spiral down into despair

Weeping with sadness
No one to turn to
I hug myself
And hope tomorrow never comes

Star Gazing

Tonight I sat out and I looked up
Star gazing into space
Watching the moon pass through the wispy
velvet clouds
An eerie glow

Not a sound, not even a whisper
Just a merest gentle breeze keeping me company
through the night
A night where I wandered through time and
space
And I never moved
And yet I was moved

Private Investigator

Dark corners glow in the middle of the night
Their stark shapes silhouetted by the moonlight
Under cover of darkness I stalk my prey
A shabby rain coated chain smoker
I move from street to street
Chasing long distant wailing sirens that never
seem to silence
Unfriendly strangers stare, and then disappear
into the night
As I continue to follow my only lead
Down town along cracked pavements and
homeless blankets
Colourful flashing neon signs and 20 percent off
Just as I'm about to turn in for the night for
black coffee and gin
There she is
Red lipstick and high heels clattering
All across the pavement and graffiti walls
What a way to go
Gun still smoking in the road
And down comes the rain
To wash us all away

Orphaned

You have PAIN written all across your face
I feel it flowing out of you
Deep and gushing
Like you have never known light, colour,
warmth and love

You stand in front of me
Carved in stone
Weathered; a product of terrible times
Dark and damp, biting cold

What can I do to change this?
To bring you back from the depths
To thaw this desperate chill
That seeps out from your eyes

Tired of time itself
Light from a flame
Tire of time to heal
Lasting embrace

163

Sunset Daydream

Looking into the distance
I see a strawberry sky
Setting into the distance
Going down behind the hill
Glowing into the distance
Behind many flocks of birds
Beyond farmland
And a windy river lost in the distance
Going down red dream
Like from days past, distant
As I stare into the sunset
Feeling strangely homely in my town

Empty School

An empty shell
Of marble halls
A hollow home
Slowly falls
Pins drop
In corridors
Paint cracks
In summer heat
Stillness reins
Quiet feet
Whispers past
Ghostly gone

High Rise

The skies the limit
In parallel worlds
Packed in like sardines
Concrete and glass
Glistening in the heat
Graffiti melting inside
Grime and endless stairs
Towers make their stand

Hummingbird

Ripple out
Silent ghost
Humming bird
Mortal soul

Ripple out
Twilight ends
Rivers glass
Semi-glow

Ripple out
Nectars thread
Common path
Gardens flow

Ripple out
Rainbow colour
Sun and rain
Pastures roll

Ripple out
Breath of air
Fields of dreams
Humming bird go

January Days

Dull dark dismal
Cold clam chill
Grey gripping grime
Seeping into all my cracks
Bringing me down
Gloom

Sinking Stomach

Slipping down into my sinking stomach
Turning in on itself
Gripping me with the fear of my own existence
Guilty cramps
Forcing me to look in the mirror
Not liking what stares back, trapped
Turning away

Turning Tides

A gentle flow on the river bend
Ribbons flying on the wind
Clouds climbing high
Tractors trudge through muddy fields

In the distance a sun goes down
Disappearing beneath a hill
Taking away the light
Giving us the night

A sparkling sky of jewelled stars
Winking at each other across the cosmos
Planets slowly turn in tune with their moons
The moon turns the tide

Seas roar with wild wind
Across an ocean made from cloud and rain
Rain that falls over sea and land
Rivers that gush an ocean beyond

Witches Wedding

Witches wedding, broomstick bride
Deep inside the forest, where you hide
Small homely cottage, cauldron bubbles away
Let the people gossip and say what they say
Fine dress of black, long golden hair
Captured by her beauty, he couldn't help but
stare
Together they danced, together they sang
All through the forest, their magic music rang
Falling for each other, the unwritten code
High in the night sky, on her broomstick they
rode
Holding her close, holding her tight
Overcome with love, during the night
Owls did hoot, wild beasts cry
To the witches' cottage, all beasts fly
Gathering around the cottage, protecting it from
evils
All beasts were present; owls, wolves, even
weevils
The sun in the sky, the waking of dawn
The two emerge from the cottage, and love was
born
The animals raced away, this way and that
Lots to be done, in just a few hours flat
She knew what would be, the lovers separated
by deer
A first lingering thought, but all was clear
Led away from her, he could only guess

Alone and naked, she waited for the dress
Bathing in the stream, so clear so clean
Could this really be happening or was it all a
dream
Carried by many birds, through the forest of
trees
It glides over her body, ending just below her
knees
Shimmering cream silk, worked on by many
Beautiful girl of magic, healing hands for any
Crown of wild flowers, trailing natures scent
Now she walks the walk to where only a few
before her went
Mighty forest stags guide her to a sacred place
Deep inside the heart of the forest, at last face to
face
There her man waits, by an ancient alter
Displaying fountains of fire, and colourful
flames of water
Clad in black robes, mystical and broad
Carried by eagles, it's the legendary sword
The two stand side by side, before the forest
prince
Some of the animals turn, while others painfully
wince
As the swords blade cuts the two, a cup collects
their blood
They drink to each other, love flows in a flood
Sparrows bring twine, from the mightiest forest
tree

Which binds their hands together, so in each
other they will forever see
The prince bows his head, his antlers hold two
rings
Each place the others ring and the animals
rejoice and sing
At last they kiss, and to the prince they bow
Waving to the gathered, all the fair and foul
Hand in hand, they walk back
Away from the alter, down the secret track
Back to the small cottage, glad to be alone
But not for too long, for many had followed and
flown
That night the two joined in love as one
And a very special magic by her to him was
done
Emerging the next morning, to be greeted by all
From the skies to the earth, magic did fall
As they both are engulfed by a colourful flower
blizzard
For celebrating the union of the witch and the
wizard
And they laughed and they danced, singing loves
enchanted song
Deep inside the forest, they lived together
happy, age long.

Spirited Away

White purely gates
Calling out to me
An out of control, lost soul
Spinning away, spirited away

Rivers run beneath me
Grabbed by the hand
Don't grieve for me
Spinning away, spirited away

Red and green of colours seen
Lost in clouds country high
One last goodbye
Spinning away, spirited away

Reaching up, looking down
Rebirth glowing soul
Rainbow flowing centre earth
Spinning away, spirited away

Stuck in the System

Waiting in a queue
Waiting for my turn
Slowly moving along
Waiting its turn
A long way to go
In the queue
Waiting, just waiting
Checking to see
I's to be dotted
T's to be crossed
Won't be long now
I'm sure to be next
Waiting in a queue
With everybody else

Abandoned

No one wants me
No one cares about me
Sitting on the cold pavement
Staring into space
While all around me the world goes by
No one sees me
Invisible
A ghost
A stain
Eventually moved on
To another cold pavement
Staring into space
As the world goes by

Escalator

Escalator goes up and down
Round and round and round again
Endless feet clatter on and off
Going up going down coming on coming off
All day and all night
Endless procession of endless feet
Taking them somewhere
Continuing their journey
Only to return them again to the up and down
and round and round
Again and again and again

Unknown

I am scared and I am frightened
In this state of the unknown
I fear to know the truth
I fear not no know the truth
The consequences could be lengthy
They will affect people's lives
Harmony
But I am powerless
We are what we are
Imperfect
Vulnerable
Greedy
Nothing stays the same

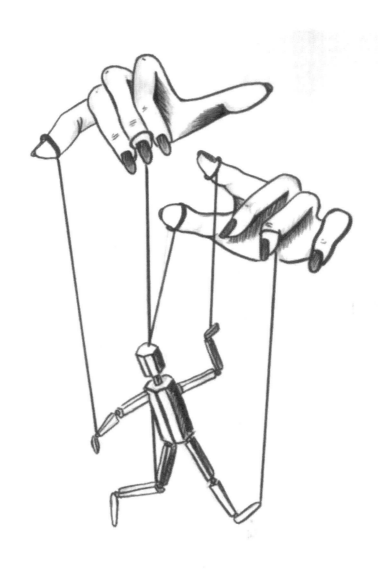

Sheep's Bleat

I am following them
They are following me
Can't make a decision
Can't think for myself
Smile at everyone
Taken for granted
Stabbed in the back
Left to fend for myself
Turning around
Seeing who's there
Waiting for something
Twisting and turning
Nightmares in the darkness

Down in the shadows
Down in the depths
The only glow

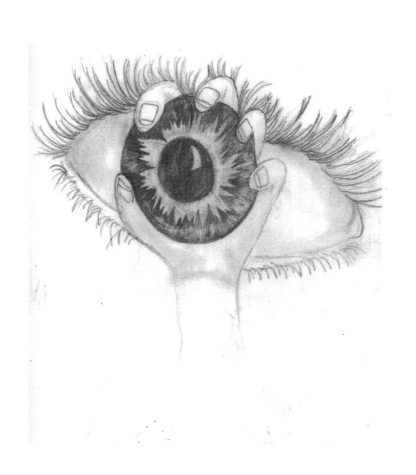

Ever Decreasing Green

There was once a field there
Now there are flats
There was once a field there
Now there is an estate
There was once a field there
Now there is a car park
There was once a field there
Now there is a town
There was once a field there
Now there is a road
There was once a field there
Now there is a shopping centre
There was once a field there
Now there is a concrete jungle
There was once a field there

My Artists

Pencils and pens and paint on fire
Their busy minds never tire
Scratching the surface
Smudged by little fingers
With great ideas
Princess and demons, dragons and butterflies
The where's and why's
Floating up to the heavens
Drowning to the depths of hell
With mud on their trousers and ladders in their tights
They return each week telling tales of darkness and light
And they would stay, painting, sketching, writing until night
Even if they were hungry, thirsty, tired or dirty
If I did not kick them all out at 4:30!

Dragonfly

Glitter of wings
Glowing colour
Clear water skater
Ripple out to all sides
Insect antenna
Join together in the reeds
Hum of wings
Cathedral

Swing

I see a swing in my child's eyes
Remembering when I was young
Back and forth, swinging
Drifting through time
Without a care in the world

I fly high and swing low
Timeless
Just at one in peace
Me and my swing
Rocking chair

People come and go
The world fly's by
All going 100 miles per hour
Yet I am happy
On my swing

The Music Sounded Like This

White marble envelops
Cascading through my pours
Touch my body
Tingle in my brain
Take me to such a high
Looking down on the perfect crimson gown
Flowing through the valley
Such wonder of god
A big bang

Movement in breath
Swaying this way and that
Bringing life to the lifeless
As the chords strike

Days old eagle stare
Drive the sane
But don't ask me how or why
Saying another story
Like an angel in my life
You come and go
This is the bitterest blow
The taker and the giver
The giver and the receiver

Patterns of symphony
Technicolor in splatters
Rainbow duel in the sky
Where sun and rain fly

Fairy lights in bubble bath
Raindrops below
Childlike joy

Fading in the corner
A passing memory
It'll come and go
Going down with the days
Whirlpool

In the city of pain
Hard cuts deep
Thorn bush prickle
Where the spikes wait
Vertical structures get in my way
Can't let out my emotions

Distant plains shape civilization
Just going with the flow
Racing backwards
Surrounded by barbed wire
As plastic people walk on by
High heels and designer labels

I see you through the gloom
Sacred prism of light
It touches my soul
Bounds of love that rip from my heart
Touching you
Deep spirits of my dreams

Centre of gravity
Quiet at times
Sitting in my field
Among the wild flowers
And the dive bombing bumble bees
Smell the sweetness of nature's harmony

Gentle child
Playing in a glade
Not a care in the world
I am here for you

The kettle whistles
Lipstick on my color
Comb your hair
Massage your back
Comforting me
You smash my cup
You cut me off
We row and argue
I still love you
Always there
In my arms
Can't bear life without you

Down the plughole
Swimming with the rats
Down the pipes we twist and turn
Splashing out the in pool of broken dreams

Harsh woolen warmth

Blow winters cold
Itch you can't scratch
Now a rash
On new skin
Dark never-ending winter gloom

Take to flight from mountain top
Peirce the sky
Soar above rugged terrain
Terrifying height
And dive
Dive at frightening speed
Shaft of light rips through
In your domain
Lord of towers high

The pier on a sunny day
In black and white
Children bounce beach ball
Couples bathe under umbrella
Sun glides over the beach
Dogs run after thrown driftwood
Splash in the tide

Haunting memories
Wail of the gull
Crabs in rock pools
Preaching in the nearby church
Historic ruins of the past
People walk on by

Café in the capital
High class cliental
Sky high cash
Coffee and cream
Art deco
Shapes slide and angle with design

Gentle glitter in tears
Finding a delicate flow for all those years
Take my arms and wrap around
For you have me and I have you

Looking away from the dirt
Pretend it isn't there
Walk on by
Disappear
To where others mooch
Following them somewhere
Part of the flock
Sheep

Playing in the garden
Growing things that fade
Let life be your drink
The quench your breath of live
From seed to flower
From baby to brother

Faces everywhere
Some fair some foul
Where do they all fit in life's epic story?

Where do they all come from?
Where are they all going?
Strangers on the street
Too many to know
Our billions of unknowns
Faces everywhere

Take away these days
All that I can see
Where has all the love gone?
Let these days go and never return
Time elapses too slowly
And my day is never in sight
My day is everlasting night

Christmas shiver
Under the tree
Needles falling on the carpet
Family together and apart

Raindrops on the window
How they race each other to the bottom
Shower in the spring
Dripping wet garden
Grass cut to fit
Window misty with breath
Drawing a face with a smile
Rain hammers down for a while
Until then I sit and stare
It can rain all day for all I care

Two sides to a person
Beware the knife in the back
Betrayal
Trust

I see the day
I see my fate
I go unsure
I hate to wait
I travel without care
I hate my life
I see people I like
As I search for a wife
I smile and grin
I shake many hands
I hold my tongues
I eat and drink
I want to shout

Wave crash from seas on distant lands
Slip like grains of sand
Your life lies beyond
To exist with grief
Take my hand and come with me
Open your eyes
And I'll make you see
A life of precious gifts is within your grasp
End this charade, this sorry farce
Just reach out and touch my face
A life beyond, beyond this place

See the robin dancing in the snow
See the deer through the trees
See the foxes playing tin the field
Hear the song of nature's melody
Come with me into a land of music and song
Where you and I and they belong
Where you'll never want for anything again
As you drink this bounty of driving rain

Rejoice at the happiness of life
This is god's greatest gift
Sing and laugh and dance and smile
Dancing round and round
Lost in a world of joy and eternal happiness
The world's one big smile

Dancing through the fields, woods, villages and
valleys
All over the earth
All you boys and girls and ladies and gentlemen
Dance the dance of joy
Sing the sing of happiness
And feel the gift of love and life
Forever in your hearts
For the music sounded like this

Millie Matthews

Melting Sandcastles

Early spring sprinkled
A few days away
In early spring
Wrapped up warm in a topsy-turvy house
The wind howling along the narrow sand-blasted
streets
Waves crashing in, one after another
Quiet contemplation in the quiet room
The room with a view
Seashells decorated sandcastles
Slowly melt into the sea
Seagull's alarm clock wailing
Lighthouse guiding light
A mixture of arcades and art galleries
Surf shops and more art galleries
Full up car parks
Fish n chips
Buffeted along the empty beach
In fierce winds and rising foam
Yet all is tranquillity and warmth
Not a care in the world
For we are on holiday
A few days in St Ives
Where children's dreams live
Inside melting sandcastles

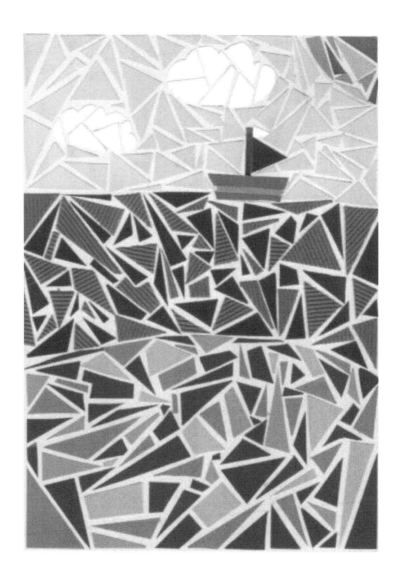

Our Special Place

The weekend
Time spent at home
Decorating our living room
Stripping away the layers of years
Putting on a fresh face
With a splash of paint
A new dawn
A new day
Worth sacrificing the weekend
For our special place of warmth
For our special place of love
For our special place we call home

Sometimes a glass of wine
and a friend is all you
need.

War Child

Tears raining down
Drowning out the days
War child
Children without dreams
Only nightmares
Caught up in conflict
Lifeless is the endless fire
War
Where bones turn to dust
Behind barbed wire fences
Faces on the dust
Unrecognizable
Lost in the wind
Forever floating away

The Great Jigsaw

On the horizon
My band of brothers and sisters
Come to me
Stumbling over the threshold
With pale faces and torn hands
Eyes wide with loss and fear
Tears flowing, silent whispering
Lost and unloved
Staring into space
Trying to understand
Of where and when and how and why
They somehow somewhere fit into the great
jigsaw
That is life

Jellyfish Harpoon

Energetic biorhythms
Captured in tune
Propulsion through the depths
Glowing in the dark
Sparkling in the sun
Glinting whirlpools funnels
Air bubbles floating away
Sucking out the venom
In deep coral caves
The sun's rays raining rainbows
Shoals gather and scatter
Guided torpedoes
Top and bottom of the food chain
Blue lagoon
Under Atlantic flow
Over pacific flow
Life and colour and deep in blue

Rain

Crafted by eons of breathlessness
And the seas roll in
Crash and bash mighty rocks
And rain

Coastal paths engrained in memory
Passing by ships and wild flowers
Crumbling chimneys of ancient tribes
And rain

Soft sandy beaches
Melting sandcastles and bright colours
Wild rugged countryside
And rain

Bright summers
Dark winters
Blooming springs
And rain

Rain and rain
And rain and rain
And rain and rain
And rain and yet more rain

Rain that drenches
Rain that splashes
Rain that floods
And rain

I really want to love this county
There is so much to it
So much history and so much beauty
And so much rain!

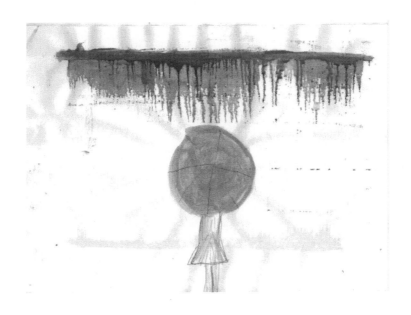

For King and Country

I saw him below me in the gathering
My eyes somehow drawn to him
He just seemed to stick out somehow
More than any other
He had the face of a man that knew he was about
to be slain
And yet there was majesty about him
An air of 'forever England' that surrounded him
For king and country
A supreme courage that would stand between
him and the enemy
That they might know his face, his eyes, his
being
As they spilled his blood and took his life

And yet killing him only made him stronger
For his he became legend
And long after, centuries after
Statues were revered
Kings and queens knelt before him
Generations came and went
His ideals his policies, his beliefs
Still they were practised
Until legend became myth
Myth became fairy story

Fairy story became forgotten

Ancient ruins
On a distant hill
A shell of what was once
Great castle and cathedral
Whistling wind
The sound of the dead
Still swaying and gliding with their king
On the wisps of the mist
That surround eternal

Trethevy Quoit, potal dolman, St Cleer

Neolithic dolman dating from 3,500 - 3000 BC. Capstone 4.2m long,
and weighing 10.9 tonnes.
Chamber formed by six stones, one is a dividing slab between
the main chamber and a small forecourt fronted by two uprights
(one now missing) A rectangular piece cut from the lower corner
of the dividing slab, gives access into the chamber.
Once surrounded by a stone cairn and covered in a
mound

Flying in the Darkness

In the cold dark bleak winter
Flying through the darkness
The deep and winding lanes
Tracks in mud and dirt
Where dirt did fly
Up and down the hills
Where the wind flows and rain pours
Still the cycle continues
Its relentless pace
Flying through the light and dark
Back and forth
Until the day is done

Following the stars
Guided by specs of light
Across the land at searing pace
Until blinding light
Dawn of day
Hiding in dark places
Cowering until sleep
Taken to another world
At snail's pace

Dreamland
Guided light

Past villages and towns of cruel stares and bitter
spite
Cracked houses cracked windows
Broken fences and overgrown fields
Miserable animals moaning for more
Clawing at the undergrowth to get far away
Under the moonlit lanes
Under the moonlit rivers
Under the moon

The dawn wind stirs
Guiding the wheat to flow this way and that
Playing with it
While in the distance windmill sails turn
The cockerel heralds a new day
He stands proud on the barn roof
Letting us his rising call
And all around us we scatter in the day
This way and that

Around the next bend
Across the rivers stepping stones
A new world is bathing in sunlight
Over the brow of hills
Sunny side up
So where now in this bleak world?
Another day to hide

And wait for the night sun

Hated by so many
Drained by so many
Hunted by so many
Was it my eyes? So black and all seeing
Was it my clothes? So black and misunderstood
Was it my teeth? So long and so hidden

Struggling to keep it all together
Writhing in agony
As my thirst for blood engulf me
Twisting and turning in slumber
Until I sit bolt upright
It's time for another
Time to drink
Or I will go crazy
Now just praying for the night

Shooting star glides across the heavens
Like it want me to follow
And I do
Like a ghost in the night
Until the farm appears
And there she is
The milkmaid
Humming a happy tune

Not a care in the world
Until my black veil falls

Escape into the darkness from where I came
Full up
And now I fly
Flying in the darkness
Flying to anywhere
Just to get away
To put enough distance between me and the
farm
Before the torches are out
Lighting up the village for revenge
But I will be far far away
Lost and alone
Hiding under bridges
Lost, in deep dark dank tunnels
Eyes wide looking
Ears pricked listening
For the many who seek me out

Sitting in the pressing gloom
Thinking why me?
What did I ever do to deserve this?
Why do I have to keep running?
Why do I have this power and with it this
burden?

Will I ever be free?
Will I ever know love?
Will I ever have the warmth and safety of a
home?
Or am I damned forever
To live a life always running
Until one day I can't run anymore

The Day That Never Comes

And I stand here
Bear with me
Briefcases walk past
Polished shoes

I will stand here
You will pass by, farewell
And I see you go
Glittering sky

Streets flood
And she'll pass by
And he'll walk past
Pound signs

Tears fall
Rain drops
Showering down
Pound notes
Shivering, wounded
Am I unlucky?
And she walks on by
Shall I

Homeless
Shapes under blankets
Rolls Royce rolls by
Glistening

Walking by
Walking on
Money everywhere
Moving on

Silently rushing
Past us all
While others sleep
In doorway halls

The bitter cold bites hard
Turning my blood to ice
Aching in every pour
Until it's too cold to move and too cold not to
move

Paralysed
In-tune with the moon
And all too soon
I can't close my eyes

Adidas walks by
Nike runs past
Who's next?
Ripped jeans

Pounds and pence
Them and us
Staring at my empty cup
Until it drops out of my hand

Another day
Another wall
Another pavement
Nothing ever changes

One day things will change
One day people will care
But at the moment
That day never comes

A cold stare
That couldn't happen to me
Get up and get a job
Take my hand

We're All Mad Here

Down the path and into the woods
She skips along with her basket of goods
Follow the path if you can
Lost already, this was not part of the plan
Round and round around and down
Deeper and deeper away from her town
Where the flowers talk and magic creatures roam
Lost in the forest far from home
Weeping all alone on the floor
When all of a sudden he appears from an open
door…

Why it's the Cheshire cat
"Don't cry little girl let's have a chat"
With a large grin and soft purple stripy fur
He curls up next to her and begins to purr

"What's your name little girl?"
She looks up and brushing away her tears she
does a twirl
"Claudia" she says in a little voice
"You remind me of Alice"
"She is just beyond those trees playing bowls at
the palace
With the Queen of hearts

"OFF WITH HER HEAD!"…"Err, Maybe later"
"You can join her once we've had lunch with the
mad hatter
Oh come on Claudia what's the matter?"
"I'm lost in the woods…how will I ever find my
way out?"
"Just follow me, to there and back again"
And with that it began to rain

The Cheshire cat climbed high in a tree
Placing into Claudia's hand small golden key
But before she unlocked and walked through the
door
The Cheshire cat changed colour to green
Then he could not be seen
"Oh you silly Cheshire cat"
And then he was wearing a hat
"There he is high in the tree
He speaks in a whisper then as loud as a bee
He speaks in riddles, puzzles and twists and
turns
He sings he laughs he jokes he learns
And just when you think he's gone, he jumps out
He beckons to you with a shout
He leads you up the garden path
He says things that make you laugh
He's my favourite cat in the entire world

As he grins and purrs on my lap curled

Claudia walked through the door
And found herself safe on her bedroom floor
"Oh what an adventure I had" she said gazing
outside at the stream
And all I have to do, to see him again, is dream

Glow

Teaching knowledge
Until they get it
Sunk in
Stuck
And for me
Afterglow
In my soul

White Noise

Spirits signal
Dots and dash
Matrix mystery
Inky black corners

A telephone crackle
Alien sound
Disturbing harmony
Question marks

Unrecognised melody
Clash and crash
Beep and bop
White invader noise

Headphone jack
Electronic pulse
Heartbeat overflow
Insect code

Insert speech
Catastrophic error
Alarm bells
Overload meltdown

Hum
Distant hum
Constant hum
Webcam eye

Computer says "NO!"
Red diode glow
Error code
Crash

Off button
Calm
On button
Stress

Information superhighway
Gridlocked
Noughts and ones
Binary bible

Above the clouds

Above the clouds
Where we fly
Passing over from tomorrow
To days new dawn

Open space
As far as you can see
Just fluffy white clouds
Below blue sky

Midday haze
Light breeze
Shimmering horizon
Warmth

Sunset colour
Memories glide
Falling asleep
Fade

Glowing bright
Streaming stars
Cradle in dreams
Passing on

Desperate skies
Stormy sea
Beyond the night
Restful days

Across the streams

Melodies floating in dream
Across the streams
Landscape of delicate beauty
Thrown down through ages endless flow
Sun and moon blown down
To grace the child of our day
Gazing into the distance
For the promise of time
From me to you
Across the streams
A breeze blown

Blossom

Colour floats all around
From scented blossom
Carried by summer breeze
Flowering trees

Those Endless Summer Days

Glow down on me
As I rise and fall
As April and May spring into bloom
Nectar surrounds me
Days are long
Lambs bleat
The heat hammers down
June in the dunes
Unforgiving and giving
As we splash at the beach
An essence of warmth
Running in and out of the sun
Sitting out at lunch
A white of wine
A salad bar
A glourious July red
Hiding under an umbrella
Welcome shade
As we lay in a glade
Staring up into endless blue
Making animals out of clouds
Lost in fields
Buttercups
Lost in wheat
Never wanting to be found

Flame filled furnace
High rise in August
Drought is the shout
The sound of distant church-bells
Guiding me home
The village green
Leather on willow
Batting and bowling
Jumpers for goalposts
Hanging baskets bloom
Village cheer over a pint or two
Staggering home from the local pub
Shine and shimmer sultry September
Bathe
In those endless summer days

Those Gone

For those gone
For all those we once held close
Family and friend
You are not forgotten
And though we may weep sometimes
Remembering glourious you
We do not forget
For although we may not be able to see you
Speak to you
Or hold you tight
Your formidable spirit
Your enduring presence
Your love for life and laughter
Lives on in all of us that were left behind
Forever remembering you

240